Gordie Howe

My Hockey Memories

A FIREFLY BOOK

Published by Firefly Books Ltd., 1999

© 1999 Power Play Publications Inc.
© 1999 Warwick Publishing Inc.

First Printing

Canadian Cataloguing in Publication Data

Howe, Gordie, 1928-
Gordie : my hockey memories

ISBN 1-55209-395-6
1. Howe, Gordie, 1928-   . 2. Hockey players — Canada
— Biography. I. Condron, Frank. II. Title.

GV848.5.H6A3 1999   796.962'092   C99-932289-3

U.S. Cataloguing in Publication Data

Howe, Gordie.
Gordie : my hockey memories / Gordie Howe with
Frank Condron.
[144] p.   col. ill.   ;   cm.
Includes index.
ISBN 1-55209-395-6
1. Howe, Gordie, 1928-   . 2. Hockey players —
United States — Biography.   I. Condron, Frank. II. Title.
796.962/ 092—dc21   1999   CIP

Published in Canada in 1999 by
Firefly Books Ltd.
3680 Victoria Park Avenue
Willowdale, Ontario M2H 3K1

Published in the United States in 1999 by
Firefly Books (U.S.) Inc.
P.O. Box 1338, Ellicott Station
Buffalo, New York 14205

Design: Kimberley Young
Photos: Harold Barkley Archives courtesy Mike Leonetti.
Beehive cards courtesy Arnold Davison,
the personal collection of Gordie and Colleen Howe.
Printed and bound in Canada.

Contents

The legendary Foster Hewitt, who did the radio broadcasts on CBC radio for "Hockey Night in Canada." Everybody dropped what they were doing when that show came on. This shot is from the late 1940s.

each and went out to the slough behind the house to glide around. After a while, she got cold and went in and I put on the other skate. From that moment on, I never seemed to have them off.

Hockey quickly became all I thought about, filling almost every waking hour I wasn't in school. I still feel that joy now when I lace up a pair of skates and step out onto the ice.

When we'd get a good fall of snow, the sloughs would build up and the cold weather would come in and freeze them over. God, we could skate, all the way from downtown Saskatoon out to the airport - seven, eight miles. On the weekend there would be an eight-, twelve- thirteen-hour game. I would go home and eat, come back and ask the score, then go out and play like I had never left.

My mother would even cover the kitchen floor with newspapers so I didn't have to take my skates off when I came in for lunch.

I was shy in school and not the quickest of students. Some of the kids called me "Doughhead," and that made me even shyer, I think. I also had a bone condition and had to hang by my arms from a door frame for several minutes every day to keep my spine from curving. Maybe that's where my arms got some of their muscle early on.

I soon discovered that all of the problems went away when I was playing hockey. My skills came

These are Bee Hive cards from the 40s.

Maurice Richard

quick and I could soon out-skate and out-play on the ice most of the kids that teased me off the ice.

Eventually, I got bigger too, as my physique started to take shape.

Hockey became a sort of sanctuary for me. I played every day when I was growing up. We had neighbors that told my mom they remember me as a boy skating for hours around a local back-yard rink by myself, repeating over and over again little drills that I invented for myself. I even invented ways to make the game more diffi-cult, which I'm sure helped later.

I would play against the side of the neighbor's shed with a tennis ball. I can remember going and banging on the window of the house and telling the guy's wife, "I need a soft one," and she would throw me a tennis ball hot out of the oven. The other one would be as hard as a brick and she would heat it up. I always tell kids now, if you can, try to handle a tennis ball. You can't force them; you have to play with them, and it gives you a very good touch. If you play up against something hard, when it comes back you have to either trap it down or chase it. So I became extremely good at trapping it out of the air so I wouldn't have to chase it.

Like every Canadian boy at that time, I loved to listen to Foster Hewitt on the radio calling the NHL games from Maple Leaf Gardens. I also remember being in every garbage can in Saskatoon looking for corn syrup labels to send away to get pictures of NHL players. There was a company named BeeHive, and if you collected enough labels they sent you collector pictures of the best players.

My hero was Red Wing star Syd Howe, because we had the name in common. I actually got to meet him (he's no relation, by the way) and carry his skates when the Wings played an exhibition game in Saskatoon before the war. The next time we met I was trying out for the team.

I'd already spent years playing on the rink and on the road before I ever got in a real game of organized hockey. In fact, I might never had gotten the chance if not for one of those curious things that happen to people every now and then. A group of kids were playing hockey on a really cold day when the ice cracked and one of the local boys went through. By the time we got him out and took him home he was quite close to death from exposure.

He caught a deathly cold. He got pneumonia

Harry Watson was one of my heroes when I was growing up. I met him once when I was 14 years old. He saw me play and liked my game.

ing off to one side as the other players lined up for food, I didn't know what the hell to do. Finally, the veteran Ranger defenseman Alf Pike said, "Come on young man," and pulled me into line. "Let's let the kid eat," he said, "or he'll starve to death."

In spite of the best efforts of Alf Pike and some of the other older guys on the team to help me along, I just got too homesick. When the guy I was rooming with got hurt and went home, I decided I'd had enough of Winnipeg, too. Lester Patrick and the Ranger coaches tried to talk me into taking a scholarship to the renowned hockey program at Notre Dame College in Wilcox, Saskatchewan, but all I wanted to do was go home.

Looking back, I guess if I wasn't shy, I would have been a Ranger.

II - Going Pro

In 1944, Fred Pinckney was the timekeeper for the Saskatoon Quakers senior club, and in his spare time, he did a little scouting for the Detroit Red Wings.

I guess Pinckney had had his eye on me for some time when he visited my father to talk about me trying out with the Red Wings. I was still only 15, and not quite old enough to sign with an NHL club, but I could become their property until they decided to trade or release me. In spite of my experience at the Rangers camp the previous fall, the New York club had no claim on me because they'd released me from camp. Pinckney gave my dad $100 to call him on the eve of my 16th birthday.

When the time came, Pinckney returned to our house with the appropriate paperwork in hand. Once signed to a try-out, Pinckney told me I would be guaranteed a chance to make

It was a grand adventure for a young guy — plus I got to play hockey.

Luckily for me, I was the baby of the team and too young to drink, one of the chief pastimes of many of my teammates. In any case, I was still kind of shy, so I steered clear of the wild side of life on the road.

The first guy I ever roomed with was a guy named Gunner Malone. He was a hell of a defense-man and a good-natured guy, but the bottle was like a nipple to a child for him. Damn, he always had girls in his room upstairs. He ran out of money one time and I had to buy him a suit — $40 — and here am I, only 17 years old. The world caught up to me in a hell of a hurry that year.

Tommy Ivan, coach of the Omaha Knights, was my first pro hockey coach — and a good one too.

The Knights' coach, Tommy Ivan, who would go on to coach me in Detroit, tried to introduce me slowly to the pro game, mostly because of my age. Sitting on the bench, however, just made me angry.

Through the first 15 or 20 games in Omaha, Tommy played me very sparingly. I started thinking to myself, "What the hell is going on here, my skates aren't even wet." Then one night we were in Dallas and one of my teammates got into a misunderstanding with one of the other players. The guy was chasing him all over the ice and I got mad and yelled, "Don't run." Then I jumped over the boards and took the guy on. I bumped his head off the ice a couple of times and the fight was over.

When I came back to the bench Tommy said, "What's the matter, don't you like him?" I just looked at him and said, "I don't like any of them." After that I never missed another shift. I was running at every damn thing that moved.

I scored 22 goals and got 26 assists in 51 games that first season. I also managed to tangle with most of the tough guys in the league and hold my own all right.

Tommy Ivan told Jack Adams in Detroit that he didn't think another year in Omaha would do me any good. He also didn't think a year up with Indianapolis of the American League would make any difference either. I was 18 and he felt I was ready for the big team. That was the last time I played in the minors.

two years before, were still around, and together with rookies like Pat Lundy and Gerry (Doc) Couture, we represented the core of a Detroit team that would come to dominate the league.

In our home opener, October 16, 1946, we met Toronto at the old Detroit Olympia. Adams put me on right wing on a line with Sid Abel at center and Adam Brown on left. Just past the midway point of the second period, with the score tied 1-1, Abel and Brown combined to send me in alone on the Leafs'

What a thrill to have one of my heroes, Syl Apps, interview me after he retired and moved on to a career in broadcasting.

III - Glory Years

1946-47

My wife, Colleen, often tells me that she can see the opening scene of my life story if it's ever made into a movie — it's me and a couple of the other rookies sleeping on cots under the stands at the old Detroit Olympia just before our first season as Red Wings. The place is pitch black. Then, on cue, the lights flick on and we start swinging hockey sticks, which we all kept beside our cots, at any rat in sight. The place was crawling with rats, and not little ones either — big Detroit rats that lived off all the food that people dropped between the seats.

It was a lot different for rookies back then.

My first NHL contract was a one-year deal worth $5,000 that included a clause stating

Harry Watson (above) was a real pro, even after he left the Red Wings.

One of my first fights in the NHL was with the Rocket (shown right). When he fought, it was for real and he held the grudge. We would spend a lot of time going at each other over the next decade.

legendary goaltender Turk Broda. He was a heavy-set guy compared to today's goalies, but he could really move and nothing scared him. With the puck lying loose about eight feet in front of the net, I took a swipe at it, sending it over Broda and into the net. It wasn't pretty; I just slapped it in. But it was my first goal in the NHL. The noise was incredible.

I soon came back to earth. It was nine games before I scored number two, and another eleven games before I notched a third.

During the course of the season, I renewed acquaintances with several of the professionals I had met back when I was just a kid in Saskatoon, including Harry Watson, the former Red Wing who was a Maple Leaf now, who had encouraged me to "keep it up."

One game, I was in Toronto and I turned blindly into the corner, which is something you should never do. Suddenly I heard Harry yell behind me, "Look out kid!" When I saw who it was I thought, "What did he do that for, he could have killed me." Two periods later, Harry did the same thing and I called to him, "Look out, Mr. Watson!" He just looked back and said, "We are going to get along just fine."

I ended up with 7 goals and 15 assists in 58 games in my first season. The team itself would finish fourth and go out in five playoff games to the eventual Stanley Cup-champion Maple Leafs. I didn't score a point in the playoffs.

Although my point production in this first year was low, I went out of my way to contribute in other

ways. I was determined to stay in the big league so I started to throw my weight around a bit, like in Omaha. I fought that first season with Toronto tough guy Bill Ezinicki and Rocket Richard himself. In one fight, with the Leafs' Gus Mortson, we started going at it on the ice, kept going at it in the shared penalty box, and then spilled into the stands where we almost sparked a riot.

Adams took notice of that also.

1947-48

Tommy Ivan, my old coach and mentor from Omaha, took over from Adams for the 1947-48 season. By that time, the stress of trying to control every aspect of the club had become too much for "Jawly Jahn," as Adams was called. He contented himself from that point on with managing the club and terrorizing the players between periods and after games with screaming sessions in the dressing room.

Although Adams was still very much around the team, the presence of Ivan helped to lower the level of tension that Adams liked to cultivate. Ivan was a breath of fresh air.

He was the best I ever had as an understanding, good coach. He never treated you like a son, but he was very fair. The friendship was sincere and everything, but he never let you get too close, because it would kill him if he ever had to get rid of you.

We also got a boost that season from rookies Red Kelly, another St. Michael's product, and Marty Pavelich, one of my teammates from Galt. We managed to finish second overall in the regular season behind the defending Stanley Cup-champion Leafs.

Early in the year Ivan threw together a line that

It was great news when Jack Adams named my old Omaha coach, Tommy Ivan, as coach of the Wings.

featured me on right wing, Ted Lindsay on left, and veteran center Sid Abel in the middle. We clicked right away. Dubbed the "Production Line," we went on to finish the year one-two-three in team scoring: Lindsay with 33 goals, 52 points; me with 16 goals, 44 points; and Sid with 14 goals, 44 points.

In the playoffs, we knocked off the Rangers in six games and went on to meet the Leafs in the final.

But we were no match for the Leafs that year with Syl Apps, Teeder Kennedy, Max Bentley and Turk Broda. That was one great team. We went down swinging in four. I did manage to pick up my first playoff goal and assist.

1948-49

With two years in the league under my belt, I was now sort of established as a strong young player with a future. Through this success on the ice, I began to overcome some of my shyness. Back in Omaha, I used to go out of my way to avoid fans seeking autographs. But as I matured, both as a player and a person, I realized this was important and tried to give everybody a bit of my time.

My life revolved completely around the club during these early years. I lived in "Ma Shaw's" rooming house with several other single players just a few blocks from the Olympia. And when I wasn't practising or traveling with the team, I spent my leisure hours with teammates, bowling, going to the movies, or going out for dinner. I spent summers back in Saskatoon, playing baseball and working with my father to stay in shape.

The 1948-49 season was a breakout year for both me and the Wings. I spent the early part of the season troubled by a knee injury, finally undergoing surgery to repair it in December. The injury kept me out of the line-up for 20 games, my longest absence through injury in my career.

When I did return, I sort of went on a tear, ending up with 12 goals and 25 assists in just 40 games. The Red Wings finished first in the regular season, the

Top photo: Marty Pavelich (top, right) was one of the good young rookies to follow the wave that included Harry Lumley (center) and me. Here Harry and Marty are shown with Clare Martin (left), who spent two seasons with the Wings before moving on to Chicago in 1950.

Bottom photo: Sid Abel (with his son) was a terrific captain. I learned an awful lot about being a pro from playing with him each night.

Speedy Leaf Max Bentley skates in alone on Harry Lumley. The late 40s Leafs were fast and tough.

first in what would become a record string of seven consecutive league championships.

In addition to my pretty good season, Sid Abel captured the Hart Trophy as the league's most valuable player and tied Ted Lindsay for third in league scoring. All three members of the Production Line were named to the All-Star team, my first selection of what would be 21 in all, and a huge thrill for me.

We took the Canadiens in a tough semi-final series, but ran up against that damn Maple Leaf wall once again in the final. The Leafs took their third straight Stanley Cup in four straight games, but it was the last season for many of their guys.

I led all playoff scorers with eight goals and three assists in the losing cause. Afterwards, Jack Adams said to the press, "Gordie Howe is the greatest young player I've ever seen," which felt pretty good, although I tried to ignore it. Coaches and GMs say lots of things to the press.

We did our best to get past the Leafs, even taking them on with our fists when necessary. They were a tough team.

1949-50

The Leafs may have been the defending Stanley Cup champs going into the 1949-50 season, but we were really the team to beat. We led the way virtually the whole of the expanded 70-game season, finishing 11 points ahead of our nearest rival.

The Production Line was still together and we gave opposing teams trouble with a strong combination of smooth passing and belligerent corner play. This time, we finished 1-2-3 in league scoring: Lindsay with 23 goals, 78 pts; Abel with 34 goals, 69 points; and me pulling up the rear with 35 goals, 68 points. The team entered its semi-final series with the fourth-place Maple Leafs as the odds-on favorite to win the Cup. The team would have to do it, without me however.

Game One of the series opened at the Olympia on March 28, 1950, three days before my 22nd birthday. The Leafs once again employed the defensive style they had used to control us in the finals the year before and were comfortably ahead 3-0 halfway through the second period.

As Ted Kennedy began to rush the puck up the left wing, I chased him from behind and picked up speed to take the Leaf captain into

My first All-Star team selection was when I was 21. They also picked the rest of the Production Line, which made it one of my favorite All -Star appearances.

I played baseball in the off-season each summer (left) until Jack Adams heard about it and made me stop.

the boards from the right. Just as I threw the check at Kennedy, he suddenly dumped the puck ahead and stopped.

People tell me — people at the game — that Kennedy butt-ended me in the face just as we col-

lided, causing me to lose my balance. I don't know what happened. I just remember hitting the boards. I crashed head-first into the dasher at the top of the boards. At the same time, our defenseman "Black" Jack Stewart, who also had Kennedy in his sights, slammed into me from the side. In the photographs I was unconscious on the ice, bleeding profusely from the head and face.

When I didn't respond to smelling salts, they strapped me to a gurney and rushed off to the hospital. In the emergency room, I was found to have a broken nose and cheekbone and a head injury that was causing blood to accumulate in my brain. I was rushed to surgery to relieve the pressure. They actually cut into my skull to release some of the fluid.

Jack Adams called my family in Saskatoon and suggested my parents should immediately come to Detroit. Back at the Olympia, the team spent the remainder of the game taking runs at Kennedy.

The doctors were successful in relieving the pressure on my brain and by the next day I was off the critical list. Obviously, I would play no part in the Wings' Cup run that year, but the doctors announced that they expected me to make a full recovery during the off-season, much to everyone's relief. Soon after, my mother and sister arrived from Saskatoon, which helped a lot.

The Wings finally beat the Leafs in that series — it was a long and nasty seven games. We went on to meet the Rangers in the Final. With the circus in town in New York at the Gardens, the Rangers were forced to play most of the series in Detroit, except for two games that were played in Toronto with Maple Leaf Gardens subbing as Rangers home ice. In spite of that peculiar advantage for the Wings, the series still went seven games.

The winner was finally decided at eight minutes into the second overtime period of Game Seven when Pete Babando scored for Detroit. I was in the stands with a shaved head wrapped in bandages.

If you ask players who have been lucky enough to win the Cup a few times which one they remember best, they usually say the first one. Well, I spent most of my first one flat on my back.

1951-52

Jack Adams rewarded his Stanley Cup-winning team in his typical fashion: he shook it up. He sent a package of players, including Harry Lumley, Jack Stewart and Pete Babando to Chicago for Metro Prystai, Bob Goldham and two others. Three rookies also stuck with the team for the 50-51 season: a tough defenseman named Marcel Pronovost, a winger named Glen Skov and a goaltender from Winnipeg named Terry Sawchuk.

Instead of messing up the chemistry of the club,

Ted Lindsay tought me a thing or two about toughness. He was a good friend too.

the changes actually gave us energy. We went on to finish first overall, again, and break the 100-point barrier, with 101, for the first time in NHL history.

It was also a season of firsts for me. The 1950-51 season was the first time in my career I led the league in scoring, posting 86 points on 43 goals and 43 assists. That total placed me one goal and 19 assists ahead of second-place Maurice Richard, the undisputed "superstar" of the NHL. It felt pretty good, as the Rocket and I were already not getting along too well on the ice.

In spite of our great regular season, the team played flat in the playoffs. Led by Richard, the fourth-place Montreal Canadiens eliminated us in a quiet six-game series in which Montreal took all three games played in Detroit. I chipped in seven points to no avail. I guess losing the scoring title got the Rocket riled up, while we were soft after steam-rolling everyone all season.

Montreal went on to lose the Cup to Toronto on Bill Barilko's famous overtime winner. It was Toronto's fourth Cup in five years, but it signaled the end of a Leaf dynasty. We all felt the era of the Wings was just beginning.

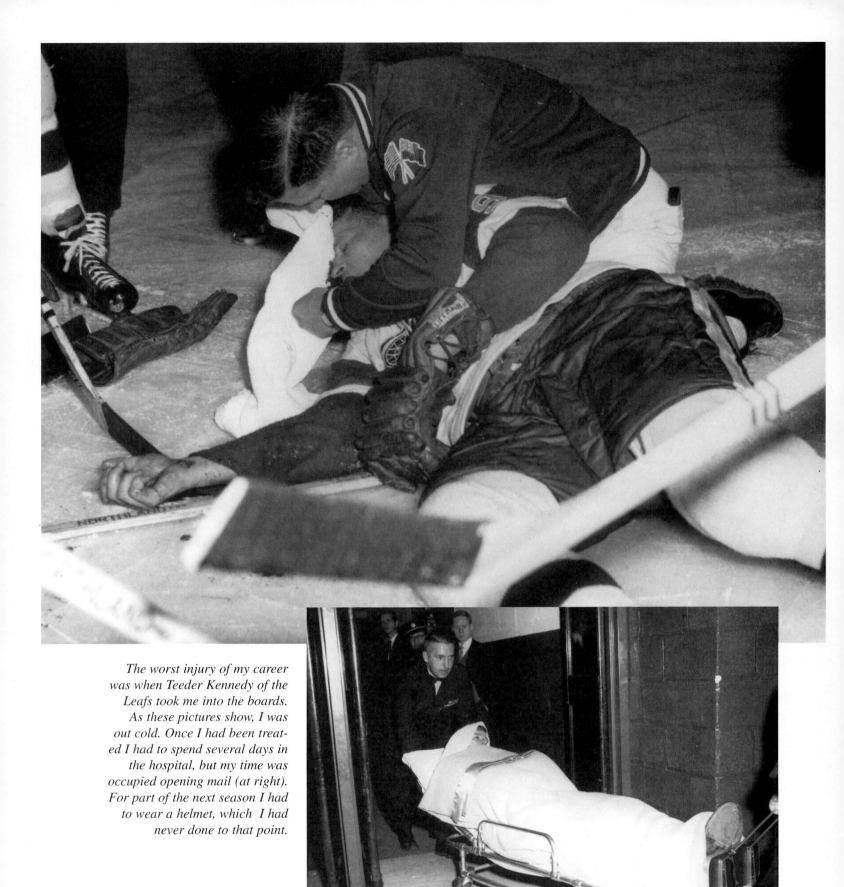

*The worst injury of my career
was when Teeder Kennedy of the
Leafs took me into the boards.
As these pictures show, I was
out cold. Once I had been treated I had to spend several days in
the hospital, but my time was
occupied opening mail (at right).
For part of the next season I had
to wear a helmet, which I had
never done to that point.*

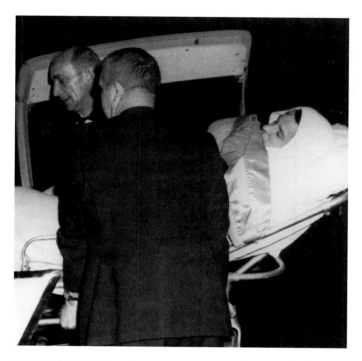

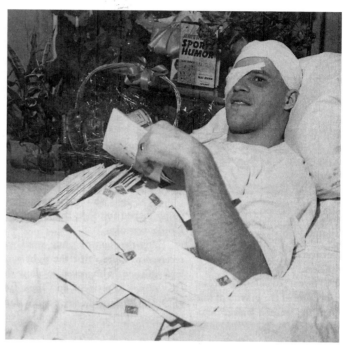

We finally beat the Leafs in a playoff series, and went on to win the Cup over New York. I watched from the stands with my head still bandaged. Clockwise, from bottom left: Marty Pavelich in the net. Ted Lindsay scores on the Rangers' Chuck Raynor. Harry and Sid enjoy the victory. At right: Harry keeps the net clean.

1951-52

We'd won the Stanley Cup in 1949-50 and had a 101-point season in 1950-51, so we felt strong at the start of the season, but there was also a lot of pressure. The 1951-52 season would be the test — would we bounce back from our disappointing playoff run, or prove to be just a flash in the pan? I think we as a team were more disappointed than anyone about our early playoff exit in the spring, and when the new season began we were more determined than ever to show our stuff.

I continued to work on improving my skills in the same way as when I was a boy. I was driven both by a love for the game and the fear that I could lose my job if my level of play dropped. It was a common fear in those days with only a six-team

league, where competition for jobs was fierce and there were always plenty of good players in the minors just waiting for their chance. I would stay on the ice long after my teammates had left, endlessly practicing moves and shots and honing the skills that ensured my place on the team.

This work ethic, as well as my politeness to authority, made me a particular favorite of Jack Adams. Above all else, Adams admired hard work, loyalty, discipline, and a fierce will to win, and the "Big Guy," as Adams called me, "delivered." So while other Red Wings, no matter how talented, always stood the chance of being dumped or moved by Adams for any reason, I remained "untradeable."

This extra practice paid off on the ice also during the 1951-52 season. I played all 70 games and

In 1951 a young guy from the prairies, Terry Sawchuk, made the team to replace Harry Lumley. He turned out to be the greatest goalie ever, setting most of the records for that position during his career.

matched my point total of the year before, 86, to win a second scoring title. This time, however, I managed to push my goal total to 47, just shy of Rocket Richard's magic mark of 50 posted during the 1945 season. It was a good season. I received the Hart Trophy as MVP of the league for the first time in my career.

As for the team, we tore up the league again, finishing in first place just one point below our record total of the previous year. Sawchuk took the Vezina as the league's best goaltender with 12 shutouts and a stingy 1.90 goals-against average. He was unbeatable.

As a team, we were not changed much from the previous year, but the few additions that Adams did make proved to be good ones. Rookies Alex Delvecchio and Johnny Wilson brought some young legs, and tenacious checker Tony Leswick came over in a trade with the Rangers.

We met our old rivals the Leafs in the semifinal, but this time things were different. Stoned by Sawchuk and a defense anchored by Kelly, Goldham and Pronovost, the Leafs didn't even manage a goal on us until Game Three. Toronto bowed out quietly in four games, scoring only three times in the series. And this was with me scoring no points and being double-teamed whenever I stepped on the ice.

In the other series, Montreal finally outlasted Boston in a tough seven-gamer, setting up the first in what would be a string of four Detroit-Montreal finals in five seasons — it was a new grudge match to replace the aging Leafs.

Game One saw us up 2-1 late in the third and Montreal pressing for the tying goal. When the announcement came for one minute left to play, Habs coach Dick Irvin pulled his goalie for an extra attacker. Ted Lindsay quickly decided the game with an empty-net goal to make it 3-1. Then, to Irvin's horror, the timekeeper announced that a mistake had been made and there was, in fact, two minutes left. They had another five or six shifts at us but we held them off. Then we took Game Two in Montreal 1-0 in a real hard-fought defensive struggle.

The story was the same back in Motor City; we scored just enough and stayed out of

Our rivals in the early '50s were the tough and talented Maple Leafs, but as their squad got older we took over. Above, the team accepts the Cup. The smiling kid at left is Bill Barilko, who scored the winning goal and then disappeared while on a hunting trip in the off-season. At left is Teeder Kennedy planting one on the Cup. He and I had an intense rivalry.

*We rolled over everyone in 1952, and this time I got to play. Above, Ted Lindsay, Sid Abel and
Tony Leswick (left to right) enjoy the hard-fought win. At right, Terry Sawchuk racked up four shutouts
in eight games during the playoffs. He was unbeatable.*

Sawchuk's way. Two more shutouts later — "Ukie," as we called him, racked up four in eight games in the playoffs — and we had our second Cup in three years.

As for me, I chipped in with two goals and five assists in the eight-game steamrollering. More importantly, though, I actually got to "sweat and bleed with the boys," as I like to say. For me, '52 was really my first one.

1952-53

As in championship years past, Adams did not "stand pat" following the '52 Cup triumph, and his most notable move affected me directly.

Our veteran captain Sid Abel was offered a chance to act as a player/coach with the bottom-dwelling Chicago Blackhawks and Adams obliged. With that, I lost just about the only centerman I had ever known in the NHL. Ivan responded by promoting Alex Delvecchio to the top line.

The next great round of rookies came in 1951 and included Johnny Wilson and future captain Alex Delvecchio (above). Alex was as steady as they come.

one of the Wings had been hospitalized — which was me with my head injury a couple of years before.

The Red Wing freight train kept right on rolling through the 1952-53 season, finishing top in the league for the fifth consecutive year. No fewer than five of us placed in the top eight in league scoring: I was first with 95 points and won my third Art Ross Trophy as top scorer, and then Lindsay, Delvecchio, Prystai and Kelly were all up there with big points.

Along with the Art Ross, I also took a second Hart Trophy as league Most Valuable Player. And my teammates grabbed a bunch of silverware also — Terry Sawchuk won his second Vezina, and Red Kelly won his second Lady Byng for gentlemanly play. Wings dominated the All-Star team, with me, Lindsay, Kelly and Sawchuk all making the first team.

There were changes off the ice for me as well. Immediately following the '52 season, Ted Lindsay married his fiance Pat, and moved out of Ma Shaw's to a house in the Detroit suburbs. We stayed friends and after a summer back in Saskatoon I moved in with the Lindsays.

Meanwhile, I had also found something other than hockey to occupy my time. During a trip to the Lucky Strike bowling alley during the 1951-52 season, I had met a seventeen-year-old secretary named Colleen Joffa. We dated off and on for several months and were a steady item by the beginning of the 1952-53 season. She didn't know who I was when we met, which was a nice thing. It was only later that she figured it out, because her father reminded her of the time he had been so upset when

The 1952-53 season would also be the year I would come closest to breaking Richard's magical 50-goal mark.

I went into the last two games of the season — against Chicago and Montreal — with 49 to my credit. Everybody fed me the puck, but I came up empty against the Hawks. That left me with an opportunity to at least tie the record in Montreal, against Richard himself, on the last night of the season.

Ivan double-shifted me the entire game, as he had been doing for several weeks, in a desperate attempt to get me the goal. I remember everybody doing everything they could to set me up, even passing up good opportunities for themselves. I felt like I was out there all night, and the guys were all looking for me. I had a few chances, but the Canadiens weren't playing to win, they were just playing to stop me.

Montreal winger Bert Olmstead was assigned the task of shadowing me and he managed to hold me to just five shots in the game. I was really disappointed, and I would never get as close again.

Maybe all the brouhaha exhausted us because we came up flat in the playoffs. The fourth-place Boston Bruins managed to upend us four games to two in the semi-final. The feat is even more incredible when you consider the fact that we finished 21 points ahead of the Bruins in the regular season and won 10 of our 14 meetings that year. We underestimated them, and they had nothing to lose. You see that a lot in sports. It must drive gamblers and bookies insane.

As for me, I barely had time to lick my wounds; Colleen and I got married in Detroit on April 15, 1953.

Pretty much from boyhood until I met Colleen when I was 23, my life revolved almost exclusively around hockey. I had always lived, traveled, practised and socialized with teammates. Now a married man with a house and soon to be a father, my focus began to shift from team to family.

Ted Lindsay's role as my best friend and the

My wife Colleen in the early '50s. We were married on April 15, 1953, and Ted Lindsay was the best man. Along with the days each of the kids was born, it was one of the greatest days of my life.

Red Kelly puts one past our old teammate Harry Lumley. He was a great addition to the team.

most important presence in my life in Detroit was now taken up by Colleen. My off-season regimen of work and baseball in Saskatoon was replaced by building a home and family with Colleen. I've never looked back.

1953-54

The team entered the 1953-54 season with a lot to prove after our embarrassing letdown to Boston in the '53 playoffs. Once again our talent and will to win powered us to the league championship, the sixth straight.

To spread out the scoring, Tommy Ivan installed high-flying rookie Earl (Dutch) Reibel at center

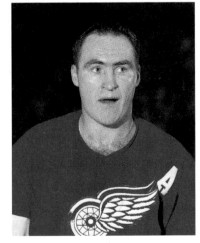

Red Kelly

between Lindsay and me and, once again, the latest model of the Production Line didn't miss a beat. I took the scoring title again, my fourth straight, with 33 goals and 81 points, 14 points ahead of Richard in second. Lindsay finished third.

But the biggest thrill of the year came on February, 18, 1954, with the birth of our first child, Marty, named after friend and teammate Marty Pavelich.

In the playoffs we rolled over Toronto in five games, while Montreal took Boston in four and we — the Wings and Habs — collided in the 1954 Stanley Cup final.

The series opened in Detroit, with us outlasting the Habs 3-1 in a fierce game that featured a nasty bout

Gerry McNeil was Montreal's goalie in the 1954 Stanley Cup Finals. He held us off for a shutout in Game Five.

Bernie "Boom Boom" Geoffrion scored two goals in Game Six, which evened this tough series at three games apiece.

replied right away on the power play from Red Kelly to make it 1-1. That's the way it stayed until four minutes into overtime.

The goal that won the '54 Stanley Cup was innocent enough. The pesky Leswick, out to shadow the Rocket, collected the puck just inside the Montreal zone and dumped it at the net just as Richard went to hit him. Leswick's knuckle ball wrist shot fooled Harvey, who attempted to knock it out of the air with his hand, and took a wild deflection off of the Montreal defenseman. Unable to react, McNeil stood frozen as the puck flipped into the net. We'd

captured our third Cup in five years. I contributed four goals and nine points in the 12-game playoff.

At the end of the 1953-54 season, the team looked to be a dynasty just hitting its stride. We had the best goalie in the league and a core of top performers in Kelly, Lindsay, Delvecchio and company, who were all just entering the primes of their careers. Clearly the first half of the decade had belonged to the Red Wings, in spite of two unlikely playoff defeats. Now the second half of the 1950s lay before us, and we had every reason to believe there would be many more Cups to come.

The happy and exhausted 1954 Wings celebrate a victory in the finals over the Canadiens. Even though we won the hard-fought series, it sent the message that our new rivals were from Montreal, not Toronto.

1954-55

While I spent the 1954 off-season fishing and enjoying time with my family, the Red Wings were undergoing changes that would affect the team for years to come.

In those days the six teams in the league were pretty much unregulated. They had a gentleman's agreement at the time to make an effort to help bolster the line-ups of the league's perennial bottom-finishers, usually Chicago, Boston and New York. Because both the Red Wings and the Blackhawks were owned by the Norris family, it was common practice for the power-house Wings to send its castoffs to its lowly cousin.

That is exactly what Jack Adams did before the 1954-55 season, except he did much better than castoffs. In fact, Adams sent our head coach, Tommy Ivan, as well as speedy forward Metro Prystai to the Windy City. With the departure of Ivan, we lost the buffer that had kept us somewhat insulated from Adams, who was tough to predict and could be hard to take on a constant basis. Adams installed junior coach Jimmy Skinner in Ivan's place, but he was viewed with suspicion by many of the players.

In spite of the changes, we rumbled on, although without the relative ease of years previous. I had what was for me an off year: notching 29 goals and 62 points, my lowest total since 1949-50 and good enough for only fifth place in the scoring race.

The regular season was memorable more for what happened off the ice than on. It was a real stick-swinging year.

In a game at Maple Leaf Gardens, I became embroiled in an altercation with a Leaf fan, prompting Ted Lindsay to whack the fan with his stick. League president Clarence Campbell slapped Lindsay with a ten-day suspension for his behavior,

during which he missed four games.

Then, after the Red Wings and the Canadiens had fought for first place throughout the season, we appeared to be on a collision course for a St. Patrick's Day tilt in Montreal to decide the league champ. A few days before the big game, on March 13, 1955 Maurice Richard got into a stick-swinging incident with the Bruins' Hal Laycoe, then proceeded to

The 1954-55 edition of the Detroit Red Wings.

punch the referee who was trying to separate the combatants. Once again, Clarence Campbell stepped in, banning Richard not only for the final three games of the season, but for the entire playoffs. The fallout from the suspension would be explosive.

We were leading 4-1 after the first period of the St. Patrick's Day game and the Forum crowd was smoldering over the presence in the stands of Campbell himself. Suddenly a tear gas canister

exploded in the stands and the arena had to be cleared, sparking a riot outside on Ste. Catharine street. Meanwhile, we had to wait in the visitors' dressing room for instructions.

We could hear the noise, but we didn't know what was going on. I remember them stuffing wet towels under the door to keep the smoke and tear gas out.

After some discussion, Campbell and Montreal GM Frank Selke decided the game would be

At a game in Maple Leaf Gardens, the Wings got into an altercation with the Toronto fans.
Ted Lindsay took a swing at a fan and was suspended for ten days.

scrapped and forfeited to Detroit. Without asking any questions, we dressed quickly and ducked out of town, tied with the Habs for first. The riot would last until Richard himself went on the radio to beg for calm.

A few weeks later, we beat the Rocket-less Habs 6-0 to claim the league title once again. It was our seventh straight first-place finish, a feat not duplicated before or since — and something that I will always be proud of — but it would be our last for some time.

Again, both we and Montreal disposed of our respective semi-final opponents, Toronto and Boston, with customary ease and lined up for another memorable final, albeit without the Rocket.

First place secured home ice for us, which we used to full advantage. We came back from 2-1 down to take Game One 4-2, and led all the way in Game

The St. Patrick's Day riots in Montreal, in which fans protested the suspension of Rocket Richard (above right).
We had to stuff wet towels under our dressing room door to keep out the tear gas.

Two on the way to a 7-1 victory and a 12-point night for the Production Line. Montreal rebounded to take Game Three at home 4-2 on the strength of a Boom-Boom Geoffrion hat trick, two of which came with me in the box. Montreal took Game Four 5-3 and the team returned to Detroit all tied up.

Back in the friendly confines of the Olympia, I matched Art Ross-winner Geoffrion with a hat trick of my own in a 5-1 Detroit win in Game Five. My 19 points to that point in the series also set a new record for post-season play. I would finish the play-offs with 20, which made up a bit for my reduced scoring in the regular season.

Back in Montreal for Game Six, the Habs refused to roll over and handed us a 6-3 loss to send it back to Detroit for Game Seven. We took the final game 3-1— and I got a goal early on.

Next to the '52 Cup — which I consider my first because I was injured in 1950 — that '55 Cup is one of my best memories because I scored the winner.

The 1955 Cup would also be my last, although I had no idea then.

Off-seasons with family were better than baseball.

IV - Milestones & Near Misses

The 1955 off-season was an idyllic one for us. Away from the rink, Colleen and I were busy creating a wonderful life for ourselves and our young family. Mark, our second son, was born in May of that year and Marty by that point was up and running into things. We spent the summer relaxing and working around our new suburban home.

My new role as husband and father had made me realize I would eventually have to start thinking about life after hockey. That year I actually went into business with teammates Marty Pavelich, Lindsay and some other Detroit-area investors, including Detroit Tiger star Al Kaline; — it was an auto parts business.

Jack Adams, of course, became more and more furious as his maturing players began to get involved in off-ice pursuits like family and investments. He complained loudly in the

Jack Adams traded Terry Sawchuk on the hunch that a rookie named Glenn Hall would be as good. Hall won the Calder that year, as best rookie in the league. Adams also named Jimmy Skinner (below) our new coach.

Angered by his weakening grip on the team, Adams decided to send the players a message during the summer following the '55 Cup victory. He orchestrated two blockbuster deals that involved half of his Stanley Cup-winning roster.

First, Adams sent his press and in the dressing room about players "pushing grocery carts instead of pucks" and becoming too wealthy off their investments to care enough about winning. Never one to court controversy, I decided to cash out my investment and concentrate on what I knew best — hockey. Vezina Trophy-winning goalie Terry Sawchuk, along with Vic Stasiuk and Marcel Bonin, to the Bruins for defenseman Warren Godfrey and forwards Ed Stanfield and Real Chevrefils. He followed that up by sending Tony Leswick, Glen Skov, Johnny Watson and Benny Wort to Chicago for

Bucky Hollingworth, Dave Creighton and Jerry Toppazzini. When we took the ice for the 1955-56 season, only nine players remained from our championship squad of six months before.

In spite of the changes, we managed to stay in contention most of the year. We finished second in the league, a full 24 points behind the Canadiens. It was the first time we had failed to finish first in the regular season since the 1947-48 season, which was my second in the league. The club may not even have finished that well if not for a Calder-Trophy season from rookie netminder Glenn Hall.

I potted 38 goals and 79 points for the year, good enough for second place in scoring, nine points behind Art Ross-winner Jean Beliveau. I also reached the 300-career-goal mark in February of 1956 when I slipped on past Al Rollins of the Blackhawks. I was just the third player in league history to reach that milestone, joining Nels Stewart and the still active Richard. From that point on, milestones would begin to take on more and more meaning for me as the games and seasons passed.

Once again, Detroit and Montreal disposed of their semi-final opponents, Toronto and New York respectively, setting up, once again, a Red Wings - Canadiens final. Unlike '52, '54, and '55 howev-

I scored my 300th goal on Al Rollins of the Blackhawks.

er, the ascendant Habs would not be denied this time around.

Led by big Jean Beliveau (19 points in the playoffs), Montreal disposed of us in just five games. I kicked in with 3 goals and 12 points in 10 playoff

We disposed of the Rangers in the 1956 semi-finals and moved on to Montreal.
Alex Delvecchio gives Gump Worsley some trouble in this shot.

games, but this time I was overshadowed in the finals by the tall French-Canadian.

The '56 Cup-winning Canadiens reminded me of the way we had looked in the 1950 season. They had the look of a dynasty in waiting with Beliveau, Richard, Harvey, Geoffrion and Plante.

Perhaps the Red Wings of the mid-1950s had the same potential, but we didn't stay together long enough to find out. Every time we put something dominant together, Jack Adams took it apart. Trading Ukie (Terry Sawchuk) was just a huge blow. He was the sort of player you build a team

around, and even though Glenn was terrific, things just weren't the same after that. It's something I still don't understand. Sawchuk could have bad nights like everyone else, but there was no one better when he was on top of his game, and that was most of the time, particularly in the playoffs.

Still, we were back on top of the league during the 1956-57 season, and looked on pace to avenge our loss to Montreal the year before and reclaim the Stanley Cup. I reclaimed the Art Ross Trophy for the first time since 1954, burying 44 goals and 89 points. I also picked up the Hart as league

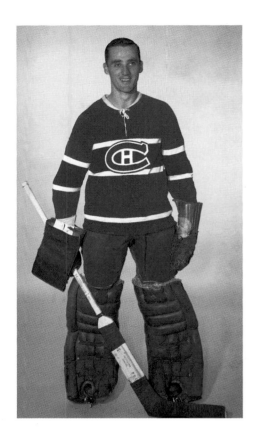

Jacques Plante (above) and big Jean Beliveau (right) were two of the final pieces the Canadiens needed to create a dynasty.

MVP, my third, and first since 1953.

In spite of our rejuvenated play, the Red Wings in 1956-57 were a team in turmoil. Early in the season, Ted Lindsay, along with veteran representatives from all six teams, had begun organizing the players into an association in an attempt to gain a voice in how the league was run and increase the players' share of the profits. Naturally, when Jack Adams got wind of the association, he went on a tirade, demanding to know from

The 1956-57 Wings look happy here but were in turmoil behind the scenes. In spite of this we had a good year. I won the Hart and Art Ross trophies for scoring and MVP and seemed to get good chances all year (at left).

each player, face to face, if they supported the movement. The tension distracted us and we bowed out quietly in the semi-finals in five games to the third-place Bruins.

During the off-season, Adams took it upon himself to rid the team of "disloyal" players. Lindsay, who had finished right behind me with 85 points in 1956-57, was dealt to Chicago along with Glenn Hall. Marty Pavelich, Lindsay's business partner, was forced to quit the NHL at 29 years of age, rather than accept a demotion to the minors.

We entered the 1957-58 season with holes all over the team, and the players that remained were all under threat of losing their jobs. I was well aware that everything I had accumulated in life to that point had come from hockey. Colleen and I had two children and a comfortable home and the

Family life was always terrific. Mark and Marty were happy kids.

The 1957-58 edition of the Wings shows some of the shake-ups that had happened during the previous year. Although Terry Sawchuk was back, Glenn Hall, Marty Pavelich and Ted Lindsay were gone.

thought of losing my livelihood was terrifying, just as it must have been for my teammates. And even if I was probably in no danger of being moved myself, it was painful for us to watch our friends being uprooted for no real reason.

With Lindsay gone from the dressing room, the Wings were left to face down Adams without their spiritual leader. When the new association filed an anti-trust lawsuit against the NHL owners, the play-ers' resolve began to crack. After a unanimous vote, the Wings withdrew from the association as a team. By the end of the season, the players' movement was practically dead. It would not emerge again for a decade.

We weren't like the players now, who stand up for themselves and who will even strike for what's right. Strikes in the '50s were almost always viewed in a negative way. It was considered an almost communist activity. We didn't have enough guts or enough leadership.

The tension in the dressing room and the fallout from the Adams purge had a devastating effect on the team. We finished the 1957-58 season in third place overall, our worst finish since my first season in the league. We were quickly steamrolled in four games by the Canadiens in the semi-finals, and they were now the team to beat.

During the next season, the wheels came right off for Detroit. Just two years removed from a string of eight first-place finishes in nine seasons, the Wings ended the 1958-59 campaign in dead last. But Adams had his revenge.

All the chemistry was gone. My own point totals had dipped but I still led the team in scoring in 1957-58 with 33 goals and 77 points and in 1958-59 with 32 goals and 78 points. But this was nothing great. I was uncomfortable with losing and getting increasingly fed up.

What made matters worse was that opposing teams

Lou Fontinato, pictured above with the Canadiens later in his career, and at top during our famous brawl. I didn't have to fight after that.

68

In October 1958 I became captain of the Wings.

assumed if they shut me down, they shut down the team. Every game felt like I was skating with a player or two on my back and a couple of sticks stuck in my hide.

All this pressure finally came to a head on February 1, 1959.

We were in New York that night, and I had been jousting throughout the game with Ranger tough

guy "Leapin" Lou Fontinato. Fontinato fancied himself the heavyweight champion of the league, and Ranger coach Emile Frances was not above sending the rugged defenseman out after the league's stars like Richard, Beliveau, and myself, to put them off their game. Lou and I had run into each other a few times over the years, so there was some history leading up to it.

That night the whole thing started with a wrestle between Red Kelly and the Rangers' Eddie Shack behind our net. I was leaning on the net, watching this lovely fight going on, and it finally dawned on me, "Louie's out here." And when I turn around, sure enough, his gloves and stick are both at the blueline,

I scored my 400th career goal against the usually stingy Jacques Plante (above) and finished second in scoring to Andy Bathgate (right) in the 1957-58 season.

and he's ten feet away and coming at me, obviously, to say hello.

I'd done my share of fighting — particularly in Omaha — and I kept an arm free and landed a couple of solid ones to slow him down, maybe stun him for a second. After that I hit him with everything I had as hard and as often as possible. He landed a couple too, but not enough to slow me down. He started bending over which is the worst thing you can do, because most guys have a lot of strength in their uppercut, so I clocked him a couple of times that way.

When we were finally separated, Fontinato was a bloody mess, with his nose spread around his face. But more than that, he would never totally recover from the fight. It's not like today when you get guys like Probert and Domi setting up re-matches no matter how bad they get beat up. When Lou returned to the Rangers, the edge was gone from his game. He was traded to Montreal, and within a few years was out of the league following a neck injury. We met up at a charity event a couple of years later and everybody made a big deal about it beforehand, but we ended up having a lot of fun and becoming friends.

As for me, I never had to fight again.

Of course, there were happy moments for me during this low period in the team's history. In October of 1958, I was named captain of the Red Wings for the first time in my career, then on December 13 of that year, I scored my 400th regular season goal against Jacques Plante of Montreal. Halfway through the 1957-58 season, coach Jimmy Skinner was replaced by my old Production Linemate Sid Abel, and then we rebounded somewhat, although not enough to make a major difference.

I finished second to New York's Andy Bathgate in the MVP balloting for the 1958-59 season, but the highlight actually was on March 3, 1959, when the Red Wings had "Gordie Howe Night" in my honor at the Olympia. With my old pal Ted Lindsay looking on, I received $10,000 in gifts, including a brand new station wagon that was driven out onto the ice wrapped in cellophane. I pulled off the

The Wings gave me a new car on "Gordie Howe Night" and when I unwrapped it my parents were inside. It was the first time they had seen me play pro hockey.

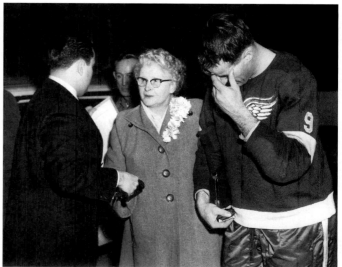

Frank Mahovlich quickly became an impact player with the Leafs. By his second full season in the League he was among the top scorers.

wrapping to discover my parents sitting inside. It was the first time my mother had been in the Olympia since my head injury in 1950 and the first time my father had ever seen me in an NHL game.

I was wishing my parents could have been there to see it, and then they brought out the car and there they were. I had no idea. It was a very emotional night for me; I broke down right there.

Best of all, on March 29 of 1959, my daughter Cathleen Jill was born, bringing the Howe brood to three.

Sid Abel succeeded in rejuvenating the team enough the next season to gain a fourth-place finish and a spot in the playoffs. We met the Leafs in the semi-finals, but they were a good club that year, led by young Frank Mahovlich and Bob Pulford up front, and Bobby Baun and Tim Horton on the blue-line. They were too much for us to handle. We got dumped in six.

The worst part was, the Leafs got a boost in their series against us from their new centerman, Red Kelly, who they had picked up from Detroit

The rejuvenated Leafs had our former teammate Red Kelly in the line-up (left) and a powerful defenseman in Tim Horton (below).

earlier in the year. In yet another act of vengeance, Jack Adams had tried to trade Kelly to New York after his star defenseman revealed to a reporter that he had been forced to play on a broken foot at the end of the 1958-59 season.

Kelly, feeling betrayed, refused to go to Manhattan and decided to quit hockey altogether.

Finally, Clarence Campbell himself stepped in and orchestrated a three-way deal with Adams and King Clancy that sent Kelly to Toronto where he had played his junior hockey.

The Habs went on to beat the Leafs for the Cup that year, the last in their amazing string of five straight.

On January 16, 1960, I passed the Rocket to become the NHL's all-time leading scorer.

I finished the 1959-60 season with 28 goals and 73 points, good enough for only sixth place in the scoring race, my worst finish in 11 seasons. In spite of that, I was still awarded the Hart Trophy as league MVP for a record fifth time.

On January 16, 1960, I passed a big milestone for me. In a 3-1 win over Chicago, I notched one goal and one assist to become the NHL's all-time point scoring leader, passing Maurice Richard. It was a position I would not lose until Wayne Gretzky came along.

To that point, Richard had 946 points in 949 career regular-season games. My two-point night gave me 947 points in 888 games. Richard would retire at the end of the 1959-60 season at the age of 39, finishing with 965 points in 978 games played between 1942 and 1960. I kept going for a while.

Family life was wonderful, but Colleen had a busy time of it with four kids and me always on the road.

Boom Boom Geoffrion (far right, top) was the star of the 1960-61 season, scoring 50 goals. We went on to the Finals that year against Chicago.

Colleen and I also added to our personal tally again that year with the birth of our fourth, and last child, Murray Albert Howe, who arrived on September 15, 1960. So, while I was "carrying the mail" every night for the Red Wings on the ice, Colleen was contending at home with four children under seven and a husband who spent much of his time on the road.

I got off to a good start in the 1960-61 season, notching my 450th career goal against New York goaltender Jack McCarter on November 6. A few weeks later I collected my 1,000th regular-season point on an assist on a goal by Howie Glover. The big night, though, came on December 1, when I got

an assist on a Murray Oliver goal to give me 1,092 total career points in 1,034 games, playoffs included. That gave me one more than the Rocket, who had retired with 1,091 total points in 1,111 total games.

The next big milestone, Richard's total goal mark, would have to wait awhile. I posted my lowest goal total since the 1948-49 season with 23, and finished the year with 72 points for fifth place in the scoring race. The star of the year was Boom Boom Geoffrion, who matched his former teammate Richard by scoring 50 goals for the 70-game season.

The Wings finished fourth, 24 points behind Toronto, who we met in the semi-final. Everybody figured we were easy pickings for the Leafs, but we dumped them in five to set up an all-American final with Chicago.

The teams split the first four games, but Chicago that season was really deep and their great offense took over. Led by Bobby Hull, Stan Makita and Glenn Hall in net (yet another ex-Wing coming back to haunt us), the Blackhawks took Games Five and Six to claim their first Cup since 1938.

I again led the way for the Wings, recording four

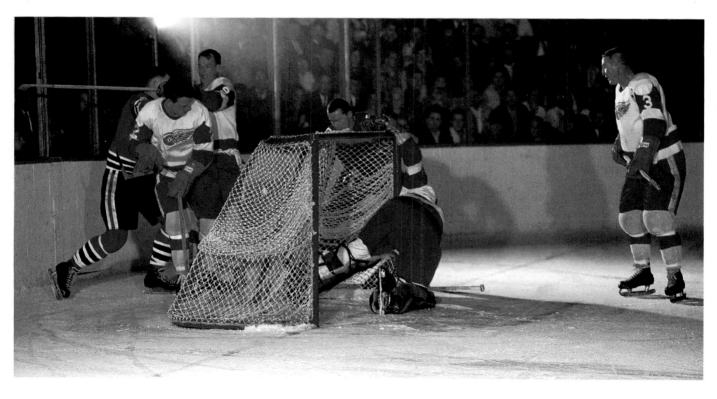

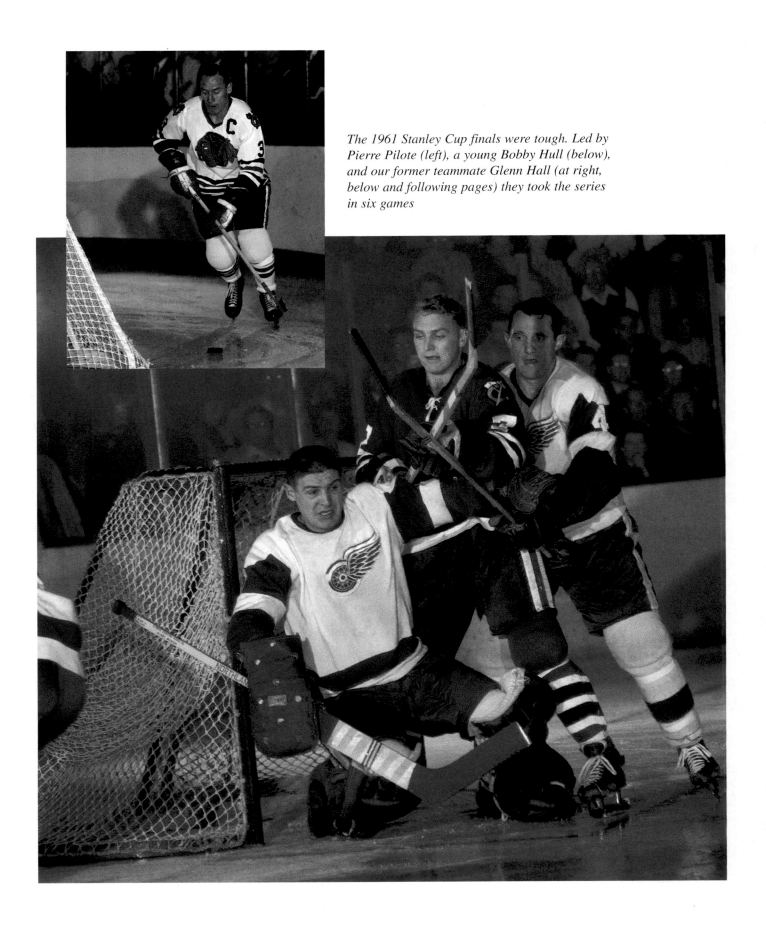

The 1961 Stanley Cup finals were tough. Led by Pierre Pilote (left), a young Bobby Hull (below), and our former teammate Glenn Hall (at right, below and following pages) they took the series in six games

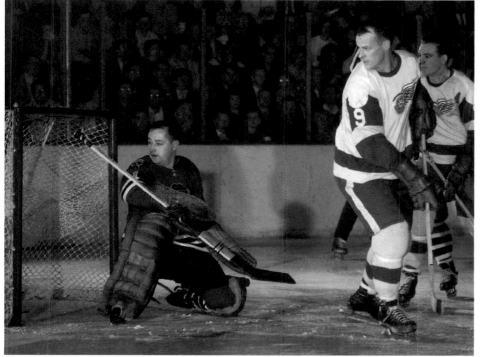

goals and 15 points in 11 games in the playoffs, and beating Chicago's Pierre Pilote for the lead in playoff scoring. I also passed Montreal's Doug Harvey during the series for the most career assists in the playoffs.

The next season, 1961-62, found us struggling again, on the way to a fifth-place finish and another early spring. For me though the milestones kept falling: the 84th game-winning goal on November 30, 1961, to break Richard's record; the 600th regular-season assist on Christmas Day; my 1,100th

I scored my 500th career goal, against Gump Worsley, on March 14, 1962.

regular-season point on January 21, 1962; and on March 14, 1962, my 500th regular-season goal, scored against Gump Worsley in New York. I would finish the year third in scoring, with 33 goals and 77 points, behind Hull and New York's Andy Bathgate. At the end of the season I resigned the captaincy of the Red Wings in favor of Alex Delvecchio.

Our unlikely appearance in the 1961 Stanley Cup final notwithstanding, the team had been struggling since getting dumped by a weak Boston squad in the 1957 playoffs, and club president Bruce Norris knew who to blame. Before the

At the end of the 1961-62 season I resigned the captaincy of the team in favor of Alex Delvecchio (above).

start of the 1962-63 season, Jack Adams was removed as Detroit G.M.; his management duties were assumed by Sid Abel.

Naturally, Adams didn't go quietly, although he was given a cushy, semi-retirement job as president of the Central Professional League. Even on his way out the door the 67-year-old warhorse continued to bluster, insisting he was being "pushed" for no good reason.

There is no questioning the fact that Jack Adams was the architect of our great Red Wings teams of the 1950s, but it is also true that his domineering presence destroyed as much as it created. Back in 1947, a good Red Wings team didn't really

begin to take flight until Tommy Ivan took over for Adams as coach. With the final departure of Adams in 1962, the same tonic worked again: less Adams, more success.

Sid Abel was relatively easy-going, which after Adams was a smart move. The 1962-63 Wings were transformed from an easy mark into a club that could compete with any team in the league. And while the team was proving itself to be a threat to win the Stanley Cup, if not the favorite, I was trying to push myself back to the top of my game.

I ended the 70-game season in March, 1963, with my 38th birthday and my sixth and final Art Ross

My old teammate from the first Production Line, Sid Abel (above), replaced Jack Adams as the team's G.M. in 1962-63, which gave me a boost. At the age of 38 I won my sixth Art Ross Trophy as leading scorer.

Trophy as the league's top scorer. I notched 86 points for the year, five points ahead of second-place Andy Bathgate and my highest total since the 1958-59 season. The 33 goals I got that year left me with a 540 total for my regular-season career — just four goals short of Richard's all-time total of 544.

We finished the 1962-63 season in fourth spot, just five points behind the first-place Leafs. We had to play Hull, Makita and the Chicago Blackhawks in the semi-finals, the same opponent that

We made it back into the finals in 1963, with great play from Bill Gadsby and Terry Sawchuk (above), and a new edition of the Production Line with Alex, me and a young Norm Ullman (at right).

had proved to be too much to handle in the finals in 1961. This time around though, our veterans, including me, Bill Gadsby and a resurgent Terry Sawchuk (who had been re-acquired to replace Glenn Hall), refused to lie down. We came back from two games down to win four straight and a berth in the final against Toronto.

We were an offense-first team, with Delvecchio and Norm Ullman and I leading the way, while Punch Imlach's defending Stanley Cup champs, on the other hand, depended on defense. With Dave Keon and Kelly up front, and Tim Horton, Bob Baun, Carl Brewer and Allan Stanley fronting a stingy Johnny Bower in net, the Leafs

Here is the early 1960s edition of the "Production Line", (left to right) me, Normy Ullman and Alex Delvecchio.

managed to keep us under wraps and took the Cup four games to one. I ended the series with 16 points to tie Norm Ullman for the playoff scoring crown. A month later, I was voted league MVP for a record sixth time — it would be my final Hart Trophy. Wayne Gretzky, with nine, passed that mark in 1989.

The team would pick up where we left off the next season, but not until I dispensed with one not-so-easy chore.

At the begining of the 1963-64 season, I needed only four goals to match Maurice Richard's career regular-season goals mark of 544. I jumped out of the blocks, bagging three in my first two games to drop the magic number to one. The tying goal proved tough to find, however.

The 1962-63 Leafs were a good club, led by speedy center Dave Keon (at left), tough defensemen Tim Horton and Allan Stanley (above, top), and the great veteran goalie, Johnny Bower.

The pressure may have been getting to me. I went scoreless for four games. Then on October 27, 1963, at home to Richard's old club, it happened. With Montreal tough guy John Ferguson in the box, our power play buzzed Habs goalie Gump Worsley. Bill Gadsby sent the puck in to Bruce MacGregor deep in the zone, who, in turn, relayed it to me in front of the net. One flick of my wrists and I had it — 544. The Olympia crowd gave me a five-minute standing ovation, which is something to experience.

If I thought getting the tying goal was tough, getting the record-breaker was even worse. Just as they had when I was chasing 50 goals back in 1952-53, my teammates did everything in their power to set me up, even to the point of forgetting they had games to win. It was a hail of passes. But in spite of the team's combined efforts, I went five more games without a goal.

The tension was finally broken on November

Gump Worsley, now with Montreal, let my 544th regular season goal in on October 27, 1963, which tied me with the Rocket's all-time tally. Bruce McGregor (above right) made the assist. A week later (November 10) I scored my 545th, also against the Canadiens, with Charlie Hodge (at right) in net. Jean Beliveau made a presentation after the goal.

10, 1963, with the Canadiens, appropriately again, back in Detroit.

This time the Canadiens were on the power play. Billy McNeill got control of a loose puck and raced up-ice toward Habs goalie Charlie Hodge. As he crossed the Montreal blueline, McNeill slid the puck over to me. I had jumped into the rush on right wing. I took one look, then snapped a wrist shot between Hodge and the near-post. Number 545 — and short-handed. Against the Habs. It felt pretty good.

The crowd went wild, this time for ten minutes. After the game, Montreal captain Jean Beliveau

presented me with an oil portrait at center ice to commemorate the event. I added a few to my total, of course, getting all the way to 801, but passing the Rocket was a big thrill. It would be a full 31 years before I would lose the title of top regular-season goal scorer, to Wayne Gretzky.

The team rode the momentum of my record right to the playoffs, where we once again ran into the high-flying Blackhawks in the semi-final. With Delvecchio, Gadsby and Sawchuk providing the leadership, it was age before beauty again, as we dumped the Hawks in a tough seven-game war. During the course of the series, I notched my 129th career playoff point, breaking yet another Richard

The 1963-64 playoffs saw us outlast the Hawks in a tough seven-game series (left and below), only to meet up with the Leafs in the final (at right).

The 1964 final was fast and furious. In the end they took us in six games on the famous "broken leg" goal by Bobby Baun (right).

record. This one without ovations, thankfully.

We locked horns with Toronto, once again, in the '64 final and the tension was thick from the start. Game One went to the Leafs on a Bob Pulford goal with only two seconds left, while we evened it up with a Larry Jeffrey goal in overtime in Game Two. The Leafs were up 3-0 in Game Three, but we fought back to tie it up with just over one minute left. It looked headed for overtime again until Alex Delvecchio snatched the victory with only seconds remaining.

The Leafs evened the series again with a 4-2 win in Game Four, but with a 2-1 win in Game Five we moved to within one game of our first Stanley Cup in almost a decade. It was not to be, however. Bobby Baun scored his legendary "broken leg" goal to even the series in Game Six and

the Leafs finished it off with a 4-0 shutout.

Ironically for me, it was the Leafs' third Cup in a row, matching the great Leaf streak of 1947-48- 49 that had stymied the Wings at the beginning of my career. For the sixth and final time in my career, I led all scorers with 9 goals and 19 points in the playoffs — I would rather have had half the points and another Cup.

During the spring of 1964, my old linemate (and roommate) Ted Lindsay was reunited with me and Alex Delvecchio in a charity game between the Red Wings veterans and the rest of the team. Although Lindsay had retired from the Chicago Blackhawks in 1960, the charity game proved he still had plenty of jump left. His old pal Sid Abel started to get ideas.

Abel managed to talk Lindsay into returning for the 1964-65 season. Terrible Ted was the final piece in the Red Wing puzzle that included a group of good young players including Pat Martin, Bruce MacGregor, Parker MacDonald and a bunch of very grizzled veterans. The mix produced Detroit's first first-place finish since 1956 and the ninth of my career.

I recorded 29 goals and 76 points for the year, but was overshadowed somewhat by Norm Ullman who led the NHL that year with 42 goals. Lindsay showed that while he had lost some of his scoring touch, notching a respectable 19 goals and 14 assists, he had lost none of his fire, adding a whopping 173 penalty minutes. He was still nasty.

I scored the 627th total goal — regular season and playoffs — of my career on November 14, 1964, against Charlie Hodge of Montreal, breaking the previous record held by, yes, Maurice Richard. It was a quiet landmark, but one that meant a lot to me. With that goal, I took the last career scoring record that remained: I now held the record for most career goals, most goals including playoffs, most career assists, most assists including playoffs, most total

points, and most points including playoffs.

But my four goals were no match for Bobby

The 1964-65 Wings finished first overall, with great play by Parker MacDonald (opposite left) and the return of Ted Lindsay (opposite bottom). Even as an old guy, "Terrible Ted" was still nasty.

Norm Ullman (at left and below) proved to have a great scoring touch, leading the League in 1963-64 with 42 goals.

Another of Rocket's records fell on November 14, 1964, when I scored my 627th total goal (regular season and playoff) against Jacques Laperriere and the Canadiens.

Hull's eight in the seven-game semi, and the Golden Jet took the Hawks into the final, only to lose to Beliveau's Canadiens. Lindsay retired for good at the end of the year, rather than go to another team.

The star of the 1965-66 season regular season was unquestionably Bobby Hull. On March 12, 1966, the Golden Jet beat New York netminder Cesare Maniago to notch his 51st goal of the season, breaking Richard's magical 50-goal mark. Hull went on to win both the Art Ross, as scoring leader, and the Hart, as league MVP. He had good speed — great speed, in fact — strength, and a killer nose for the top corner. He was also pretty tough for a goal scorer. He could take a hit and give one back a shift later.

Meanwhile, I plodded along. On November 27, 1965, I collected my 600th career goal against Montreal's Gump Worsley. On January 15, 1966, I recorded my 1,400th point in my 1,295th game. Ten days later, I played my 1,300th regular-season game. I finished the year with 29

The 1965-66 season belonged to Bobby Hull, who broke the magical 50-goal mark on March 12, 1966.

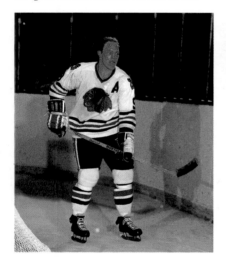

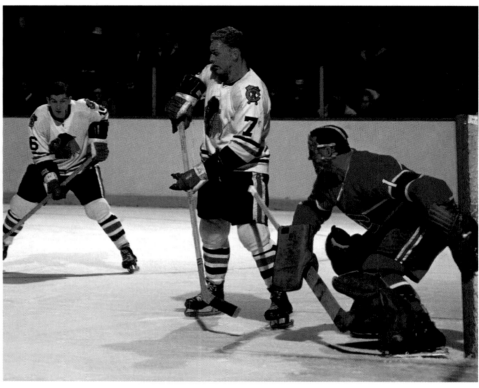

Detroit continued its string of great goaltending acquisitions when Roger Crozier entered the lineup in 1965-66.

der injury in Game Three, the tide turned. The Habs went on to take four straight to claim their seventh Stanley Cup in ten years. Crozier, who came back in Game Five, was awarded the Conn Smythe Trophy as MVP of the playoffs.

For me, the '66 playoffs would be the last chance to win another Stanley Cup. The Red Wings club would not compete for the big prize again for 31 years.

The sting of that 1966 loss in the finals was lessened somewhat when that summer the City of Saskatoon honored me with "Gordie Howe Day." A parade was held through the center of the city complete with marching bands, and us — Colleen and the kids and me — waving from an open car.

A sports complex was named in my honor and a rally was held where various dignitaries praised my career. Letters of congratulations were read from none other than Prime Minister Lester Pearson and Opposition Leader John Diefenbaker. All my great hockey adversaries sent greetings, as did my old boss Jack Adams.

The highlight of the day was the reunion, for the first time in 18 years, with my parents and all eight of my siblings. When I at last took the microphone, I was having trouble finding words. I said:

"People have been so great and kind to me... I don't think I'll ever get over it. So I just want to say once again, people behind me, thank you for all the

goals and 75 points and the Wings qualified for the playoffs in fourth place.

Although the Hawks had beaten us in 11 of 14 meetings during the regular season, we took it up a notch in the semi-final series. With a hot Roger Crozier in net, we outscored the Hawks 22-10 in a shocking six-game upset.

We took the first two games in the final against Montreal, but when Crozier went down with a shoul-

Off the ice, Bill Gadsby and I were great friends.

As the 1960s came to a close, the Bruins became dominant with the play of Bobby Orr and Phil Esposito (below).

appearances to tie my old teammate Red Kelly. Kelly, however, had won four more Cups.

Following the end of the 1970 playoffs, I had a bone ending removed from my left wrist at the University of Michigan Hospital. The wrist had been bothering me for some time, and I suffered chronic arthritis in the joint, forcing me to carry the puck almost exclusively with one hand on my stick.

If that wasn't enough, the new season was barely a month old when I suffered a rib injury in a game in Philadelphia. The injury kept me out of the line-up for the next ten games, my longest absence since missing 20 games with a knee problem in the 1948-49 season. If not for one game off in 1963-64 and another in 1966-67, I would have played 690 consecutive games between 1948 and 1971.

The boys picked up my fishing bug early.

V - Mark, Marty & the WHA

On February 17, 1971, during my final season with the Red Wings, I played in a charity hockey game at the Olympia to benefit the March of Dimes, one of our favorite charities.

The game pitted the NHL club against the Junior Red Wings, a junior-rep team started some years earlier, and with lots of success, by Colleen. At the time, the Junior Wings happened to include both Mark and Marty, our sons, aged 16 and 17. Just to help even things out a bit, both my older brother Vern, who played for a time with the New York Rangers in the 1950s, and I lined up with the kids. Our youngest Howe, ten-year-old Murray, even made an appearance late in the game and scored a goal.

With the end of my Red Wing career just months away, it was a special thrill for me to play on the Olympia ice surface with my boys and my brother. I took special delight in

hearing the public address announcer describe Murray's goal: "Howe from Howe and Howe." It sounded like a Hollywood Indian chant.

I never dreamed, of course, at that moment, that I would hear an announcer utter that line again, and not just in a charity game.

Immediately after my official retirement as a player with the Red Wings just before the 1971-72 season, I embarked on what I had every reason to believe would be a long and satisfying career with the Wings at the management level. Bruce Norris and other Red Wing executives had assured me as my career was winding down that I would always have a job with the club.

I assumed that meant some kind of active role in shaping the on-ice product, perhaps as a scout or even a general manager. Coaching, however, was out of the question. After almost 20 years of road trips, missed Christmases and media scrutiny, I promised Colleen that I would never take a coaching job after I quit playing. There had also been talk of my taking some kind of executive position with one of the Norris family's insurance company operations. The Red Wings, I thought, would take care of me.

Initially, that appeared to be the case. Shortly after I officially announced my retirement on Labor Day, 1971, the Red Wings announced that I had been appointed a "vice-president" with the club. The mayor of Detroit declared a Gordie Howe Day and the Wings hosted a banquet in my honor. At the banquet, league president Clarence Campbell declared, "Never in the history of this game has there been such an obvious and dramatic loss by a single sport... Hockey has been fortunate to have Gordie. When he came into the league, hockey was a Canadian game. He's converted it into a North American game."

Life as an executive.

Then U.S. Vice-President Spiro Agnew was in Detroit when the team retired my number.

On March 12, 1972, the Red Wings officially retired my number 9 jersey in an elaborate ceremony between periods of a game against Chicago. Colleen, three of our four children (Marty was playing a junior hockey game in Toronto) and I stood at center ice on a specially made red carpet emblazoned with a white number 9. We were joined by my dad, Ted Lindsay, and U.S. Vice-President Spiro Agnew, who attended at the request of President Nixon. I accepted the honor from club president Bruce Norris, requesting that the sweater be made available only if one of my sons ever played for the Red Wings. (Years later, Mark would eventually do just that; but, playing defense by that time, he opted for number 4.)

Shortly after beginning my new career at the

Olympia — at half my playing salary — I quickly discovered my role with the club would be anything but active. Rather than being truly vice president of public relations, as my new title specified, I remember being more like vice president of paper clips.

Essentially, my duties consisted of attending banquets and functions as a representative of the Red Wings. And even in that regard, I found I was often not informed about events and was sometimes left to make last-minute travel arrangements. The position in the Norris insurance empire also never materialized.

Ironically, it was at one of those endless banquets — in Brantford, Ontario, in 1972 — where I would make the acquaintance of an 11-year-old phenom named Wayne Gretzky. There was an instant bond between us, I remember, as if we somehow knew we shared the same rare secret. Of course we couldn't have imagined it then, but only a few years later, we would be facing off against each other in a pro game. And just over 20 years later, young Gretzky would be erasing my name from top spot in the record book.

But I quickly grew tired of being a "banquet attraction." For a man who had always been at the center of the hockey world, being removed hurt. On top of that, I had always been a man who wanted to earn my keep. I always said that I never really felt part of Detroit's 1950 Stanley Cup victory because

My duties as vice president seemed to be composed of golf games and endless banquets. I didn't mind the golf.

I had been hurt in the first game of the playoffs. During my time with the Red Wings after my retirement I felt that way again, not "a part of the team," and it made me unhappy.

Colleen described it best in her 1974 book, *My*

The boys were keen about hockey from an early age, as these scrap-book shots illustrate (facing page as well). They even made Terry Sawchuk smile, which was tough to do.

Clearly, a future in the NHL seemed a very real possibility for both of them in the spring of 1973. But under NHL regulations at the time, no junior player was eligible for the draft until after his twentieth birthday. That meant that Marty would have to spend another year in Toronto to see if he would even be drafted by an NHL team; Mark had two years to wait. The fate of the Howe family appeared to be on hold, at least for the time being.

Fate took a turn, however, with a phone call to our home that spring. I answered the phone and found my old

Three Hockey Players, when she said that all the photos taken of me were never set in my office — which was a tiny hole in the wall — but always in someone else's nice office, with their kids on the wall.

But while I was wasting away in my "non-job," events were taking place that would alter my future drastically.

Throughout the 1971-72 season, a group of wealthy businessmen led by attorney Gary L. Davidson were laying the groundwork for a professional hockey league to rival the NHL. Their plan was to place franchises in untapped or underexploited hockey markets and use big-money contracts to lure NHL stars to the new league, which they christened the World Hockey Association.

The WHA hit the ice for the 1972-73 season.

A rose between three thorns... Colleen wrote a book called My Three Hockey Players *when we started playing together. She was instrumental in all of the contract negotiations, which was unique in the all-male world of pro sports and its management.*

club more attractive to Mark, the Aeros picked up Marty with their 12th-round pick.

The initial reaction to the move in the offices of the NHL was shock, followed by panic. If the upstart league was allowed to snatch good young players right from under the NHL clubs, it would threaten the balance of power in the hockey world. NHL president Clarence Campbell was upset enough to call me at home to ask me personally to forbid my boys from signing with Houston. Not only would it hurt the league, Campbell said, it could threaten the very existence of junior hockey.

Colleen and I thought about it overnight. I was nothing if not loyal, and I was well aware that the NHL had enabled me to make a good living off my

talent. But we knew how much our boys wanted to play professional hockey, and how hard they had worked to get the chance. Now they had it. We didn't think the wait was worth it or necessary.

The next day I called Campbell back and told him that Colleen and I would not stand in the boys' way if they decided to turn pro with Houston.

Once the decision was made, Colleen and I immediately focused our energies on negotiating the best contract possible for the boys. We knew full-well by then that I had spent almost all of my career earning less than my market value, and we were determined that that was not going to happen to Mark and Marty.

As the boys grew and my NHL career seemed to go on longer (by far) than the average, it was common for other players to joke about the old man sticking around long enough to play with his sons. Now with Mark and Marty on the verge of beginning their pro careers, the idea did not seem so far-fetched to Colleen and me anymore. In a phone conversation with Bill Dineen, we half-jokingly asked, "How would you like three Howes?" Dineen said that he would love it, and he wasn't joking.

Colleen was understandably apprehensive at first. Given my age, 45, and my nagging injuries, not to mention my two-year absence from the game, the prospect of playing with men half my age was downright dangerous. But Colleen had already seen what life away from hockey could do to my spirit, and she knew how much it would mean to me to play with the boys.

After a trip to Houston to see the city and meet the Aeros' owners, we decided to give it a try. We invited Aeros president Jim Smith up to our cottage in northern Michigan to work out a deal. Colleen

and a family business advisor worked out a four-year "package deal" for all three Howes with Smith, worth just under $2.5 million. My sons and I would earn in four years what I had earned during my last 18 years in the NHL. It was like my first Wings contract — $5,000 in a year was more than my father had seen in the previous fifteen.

Twenty-five years as a professional athlete had made physical fitness something of a religion for me, and I arrived at the Aeros training camp in pretty good condition, considering my long layoff. Still, I did find it tough getting the rust off my 45-year-old frame. But I didn't care; I was back in my true element, and all the pain and gloom of the last several years faded away. The sun came out for the first time in a while that year.

The sun came out, as it were, and stayed out. Playing in 70 of the team's 80 games, I felt totally one win to Russia's four, and three ties — but the huge Russian crowds showed gratifying appreciation for Bobby and me.

I followed up my WHA debut season with a 34-goal, 99-point campaign and another AVCO World Trophy in the 1974-75 season. Shortly thereafter, the Aeros named me president, making me the first-ever playing club president in any sport. I notched 32 goals and 102 points in 1975-76 and dropped back to a merely adequate 68 points in 62 games in 1976-77.

Unfortunately, the WHA was dogged by money problems throughout its short existance, and Houston was no exception. In 1977 the team folded, and we were left looking for a place to play.

In spite of everything that had happened, we still felt that our hearts were in Detroit, and Colleen actually made a pitch to the Red Wings for the boys to play and have me come back in a real management capacity. Mark's NHL rights were held by Montreal though, and, ironically, Detroit G.M. Ted Lindsay could not, or would not, swing a deal. By this point Colleen was managing our affairs, which is probably the best thing that could have happened, as I took everything all the G.M.s said as fact, which is the first mistake. Colleen put them through their paces.

Holding out for another "package" deal, Colleen eventually signed the boys up with the New England Whalers of the WHA. This time it was a 10-year deal worth some $5 million. I was 49.

While the Howe legend continued to grow on the ice, the Howe clan was growing off the ice. Both Mark and Marty got married in Houston during the summer of 1977, and sister Cathy joined them the next summer. On April 21, 1978, I scored a goal in Edmonton and returned to the dressing room to find teammate Mark had just become the father of my first grandchild. I was 50.

Earlier that season, on December 7, 1977, I scored the 1,000th goal of my professional career, including playoffs. The victim this time was John Garrett of the Birmingham Bulls. My coach in New England, Harry Neale, said that I was so focused on getting that 1,000th goal that I would sit on the bench between shifts with my hand in a bucket of ice to numb the pain in my wrist. X-rays after the fact proved it was broken. I guess I wanted that goal.

My first season in New England, I scored 34 goals and 62 assists for 96 points. A fractured ankle caused me to miss 22 games during the 1978-79 season, and my output dropped to 19 goals and 43 points in just 58 games.

By the end of the 1978-79 season, the WHA was down to just six clubs: New England, Winnipeg, Edmonton, Quebec, Cincinnati, Birmingham and Indianapolis. The old guard at the NHL, headed up by Clarence Campbell, had been convinced from the beginning that the new league would fold quickly. But the upstarts had hung on stubbornly for seven seasons, bleeding players and profits from the NHL all the while. The last straw was the signing of my little banquet buddy, the young phenom from Brantford, Wayne Gretzky, by Indianapolis (he moved later in the year to Edmonton).

When John Ziegler took over from Campbell as president of the NHL in 1977, he immediately took a different approach. Ziegler met with his WHA counterpart Howard Baldwin, and the two decided it would be better to make money for each other rather than continue to take money from each other. A deal was reached that allowed the NHL to absorb four WHA clubs — New England (which would be

When Houston went under, we went to the Wings to see if they wanted us, but ended up in the WHA again with Hartford.

Jean Beliveau

A lot of people don't remember how tough Jean Beliveau
was when he first entered the league. He was no gentleman
in those days- big, fast and rough as they come. The fact that
he was perceived as an elegant sportsman by the end of his
career is tribute not only to the skill with which he played
the game, but also to the fact that everyone on the ice knew
he could still handle himself if the going got tough.

Alex Delvecchio

Alex and I went through a lot together. His career was almost as long as mine and covered much of the same time. Steady and motivated, he rarely missed a practice and always played at the top of his game. He was good in the dressing room also, and was captain of the Wings for a lot of the time that we played together. I think the fact that he had fewer penalty minutes (383) in 24 years with the Wings than some players rack up in a single season says a lot about his game. He played clean, good hockey.

Johnny Bower

Every time I see Johnny these days there is always some piece of memorabilia that shows a shot like this one. I always say "Hey John, I remember that play — I scored that goal," and he always replies, "Gordie, I don't think you ever scored on me, but this play I remember you shot way wide." It is something of a ritual between us. He was the last great stand-up goalie. You could be right on top of him and he'd still be standing — not like today's goalies who drop into a butterfly early and often.

Bill Gadsby

Bill came over to the
Wings from the Rangers
in 1961 and we hit it off
right away. The fact that
we'd entered the league
at the same time, and
that I'd run up against
him a lot in the previous
15 seasons, helped. He
was a great, strong stay-
at-home defenseman,
with really good balance
on his skates which
helped him steer oppo-
nents off the play. We
became best friends and
spent lots of time fishing
in the off-season.

Bobby Hull

Bobby was great to watch and to play against. When he skated past the bench you could feel his speed like no one else. And what a shot! He could get it away faster than anyone. I remember people saying that his little brother Dennis had a harder shot, but I never saw it. And no one was as accurate. He was strong too - great upper body strength - so that with his speed and accurate shot he was difficult to contain.

Ted Lindsay

Ted was the best man at our wedding and my best friend for years. We even roomed together for several off-seasons. You look at some of the gigantic kids playing hockey today — Lindros for example — and it's hard to imagine Ted at 5'10" being that tough, but he truly was a ferocious, driven, gritty player. Nothing knocked him down. Even so, he could still get the puck in the net, scoring more than 25 goals in nine separate seasons, which is always great to have.

Stan Mikita

This guy was magic with a pass, and I think he is underrated for that. A lot of the things that players like Gretzky have done come from the way Stan handled the puck. He could thread a great, feathery pass through a big crowd straight to Hull's stick.

Bobby Orr

I only got to play a handful of years against Bobby but it was an experience I will always remember. On a few occasions we got the sensation of just standing around watching what he would do next — not that we really did stand around, but he gave you that feeling. Doug Harvey had been a rushing defenseman 10 years before — which was something to watch also — but nothing really compared to Orr in his first several seasons. You really didn't know what to expect, because he broke all of the rules.

Maurice "Rocket" Richard

The Rocket and I had a fiery time of things right from my rookie season. I don't think I played with anyone as driven and determined as him, but I don't think I played with anyone as humorless either. He really didn't seem like a happy guy. Still, in terms of raw talent and competitiveness he was among the best ever, and his speed and nose for the net haven't been matched before or since.

Pocket Rocket (Henri Richard)

Not that many people realize that the Pocket Rocket has
11 Stanley Cup rings. I think he's pretty modest about
that. But he was always there, in the thick of things. He
was scrappy for a smaller guy (5'7") and he had great
speed and puck handling skills. The big thing, though,
was that he had his brother's same determination and
pride. He played to win every night.

Terry Sawchuk

Terry got a raw deal, I think, in terms of his reputation. Everyone just assumes that he was mean and nasty, which I rarely saw. His problem was that he was really shy, in a painful way, so when people started treating him like a hero or expecting him to get a shutout every game, he clammed up. Maybe it's because we're both prairie farm boys but he was always a good friend to me. Quiet for sure, but a good friend all the same.

VII - Career Highlights

(compiled by Colleen J. Howe)

March 31, 1928

Born in Floral, Saskatchewan, Canada, to Katherine Schultz and Albert Clarence Howe.

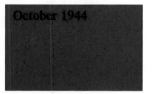
October 1943

Attended New York Rangers training camp in Winnipeg, Manitoba, and was offered a chance to play at Father Bauer's School only, so elected to return home.

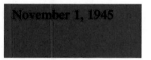
October 1944

Joined Galt of the OHA Junior A Series, but because inter-branch transfer could not be obtained, practised with the team and played exhibition games only.

November 1, 1945

Signed first professional contract, with Omaha Knights of the United States Hockey League.

October 8, 1946

Signed first contract with Detroit Red Wings.

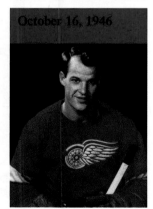
October 16, 1946

Scored his first NHL goal, during first NHL game, at Detroit against goaltender Turk Broda at 13:39 of second period. Sid Abel and Adam Brown assisted. Toronto and Red Wings tied 3–3. Howe's appearance meant the Red Wings would continue to have a Howe in their lineup. Syd Howe, no relation to Gordie, had retired after the 1945–46 season, completing 12 successive seasons with Detroit.

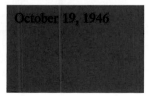
October 19, 1946

Received first NHL assist, on a goal by Adam Brown, during a 6–3 loss at Toronto. Also received his first major penalty for fighting with Bill Ezinicki.

March 26, 1947

Played in first Stanley Cup playoff game — a 3–2 loss at Toronto in overtime.

October 29, 1947

Wore sweater number nine for the first time. It was during a 5–2 Red Wing victory at Chicago.

November 1, 1947

"Production Line" of Howe, Ted Lindsay (left wing) and Sid Abel (center) became regular unit with the Wings. The three had played together the previous season but not on a regular basis.

November 22, 1947

Scored the first of 188 game-winning goals during his regular-season career. It was during an 8–5 victory against Chicago at Detroit.

January 4, 1948

Scored two goals at Detroit during a 6–2 victory against Montreal. It was the first of 147 regular-season games in which Howe scored at least twice. It was also his first of 58 unassisted goals in his regular-season career.

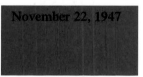
March 6, 1948

Scored the first game-tying goal of his career during a 2–2 tie with Montreal at Detroit. He finished with 30 such goals in his 25 seasons.

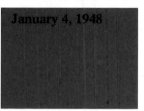

March 10, 1948

Scored two goals, including the first of 23 shorthanded goals he was to score during his regular-season career. The game, a 7–2 victory over Chicago, was at Detroit. The second goal in the game was his first power-play goal. He had 213 during his regular-season career.

April 1, 1948 — Received his first assist in Stanley Cup playoff action — on a goal by Pete Horock during a 3–1 victory at Detroit against New York.

April 4, 1948 — Scored his first Stanley Cup play-off goal. It was a power-play goal at 14:30 of the first period against netminder Charlie Rayner during a 4–2 victory at New York.

November 3, 1948 — Played in his first All-Star game. Howe wore number eleven and goaltender Frank Brimsek of Boston wore number "zero."

December 4, 1948 — Suffered torn cartilage in his right knee during a game at Boston, won by Detroit 3–2. The injury kept him out of the next 20 games, the longest period of inactivity in his career. The only other time Howe missed more than six games was in 1970–71 when he was out for fifteen games.

March 16, 1949 — Received three assists, including the 100th point of his regular-season career, during a 6–2 victory against New York at Detroit. It was his 156th regular-season game.

April 5, 1949 — Scored one goal during Red Wings' 3–1 victory against Montreal at Detroit, which sent Red Wings into the finals against Toronto. It was the eighth goal for Howe in the series. His goal total and 11 points led all players in the playoffs in 1949.

April 22, 1949 — Named to the Second All-Star Team for the first time in his career.

October 10, 1959 — Appeared in his second All-Star game, wearing sweater number fourteen.

February 5, 1950 — Scored one goal against Charlie

Rayner as Red Wings and New York tied 5–5 at Detroit. It was the first of 22 straight seasons in which Howe scored at least 20 goals.

March 15, 1950 — Scored one goal against netminder Gerry McNeil during a win against Montreal at Detroit, giving him 30 goals for the season, the first of 14 times he reached that plateau.

March 19, 1950 — Scored three goals against netminder Turk Broda during a 5–0 win at Detroit against Toronto. It was the first of 19 times in regular-season play that Howe had three goals in one game. He also had one assist, his 100th in regular-season play.

March 22, 1950 — Scored his 35th goal of the season, against goaltender Emile Francis during an 8–7 victory over New York at Detroit. It was the first of nine times he had at least 35 goals in a season. Also credited with an assist in the game, Howe finished the season with 68 points, which placed him third in scoring behind linemates Ted Lindsay (70 points) and Sid Abel (69 points). It was the first time since 1944–45 that a complete line finished in the first three places of the scoring race. The Canadiens line of Elmer Lach, Maurice Richard, and Toe Blake did it in 1944–45. It hasn't happened again since 1949–50.

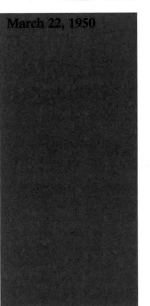

March 28, 1950 — Suffered the most serious injury of his career when he was accidentally checked into the boards by Toronto captain Ted Kennedy in the first game of the semi-final playoff series. Howe received a skull fracture and required surgery to relieve pressure on his brain.

April 23, 1950 — Recovered in time to watch Detroit

win the Stanley Cup in a tense seventh game of the Finals against New York Rangers. Pete Babando scored the winning goal after 28:31 of overtime to give the Wings a 4–3 victory at Detroit. It meant Howe was a member of a Stanley Cup-winning team for the first time in his career.

April 1950

Met Colleen J. Joffa at the Lucky Strike Recreation Center in Detroit near the Olympia Stadium.

April 29, 1950

Named to the Second All-Star Team for a second straight season.

September 1950

Brother, Vic Howe, played with the New York Rangers in the 1950–51 through the 1954–55 seasons — total of 33 games.

October 8, 1950

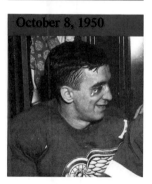

Scored one goal and assisted on one of Ted Lindsay's three goals — the first time a player had scored as many goals in an All-Star game — as Detroit defeated the All-Stars 7–1 at Detroit. Howe assisted on Lindsay's first-period tally at 0:19, still an All-Star game record for the fastest goal scored from the start of a game or period.

December 25, 1950

Received three assists during a 4–1 win over New York at Detroit, including the 200th point of his regular-season career. It was his 260th game.

January 23, 1951

Scored three goals against netminder Harry Lumley during an 8–2 victory at Chicago. It was Howe's second three-goal game in seven days at Chicago and against Lumley.

February 17, 1951

Scored his 100th regular-season goal during a 2–1 victory at Montreal against goaltender Gerry McNeil. The game was designated as a "night" for Maurice (Rocket) Richard.

March 7, 1951

Scored two goals during Red Wings' 3–0 win at Toronto, giving Howe 75 points for the season and breaking the record by a right winger, set by Lorne Carr of Toronto with 74 points in 1943–44.

March 17, 1951

Recorded his third three-goal game of the season against netminder Harry Lumley during an 8–2 victory against Chicago at Detroit. Included among the three goals was Howe's 40th of the season, the first of five times he reached that total. He also received an assist in the game and the four points gave him 83 for the season, breaking the record of 82 set by Herbie Cain of Boston in 1943–44.

March 24, 1951

Scored one goal as Canadiens defeated Detroit 3–2 at Montreal. The goal was Howe's final point of the season and he finished with 43 goals, 43 assists for a record of 86 points and his first scoring title. He finished 20 points ahead of runner-up Maurice Richard of Montreal, and led all players in goals, tying Ted Kennedy of Toronto for the assist lead.

March 25, 1951

Red Wings defeated Canadiens 5–0 at Detroit and for the third straight season, Detroit finished first, Howe being a member of each of those Prince of Wales Trophy–winning teams.

April 27, 1951

Named to the official NHL First All-Star Team for the first time, but his third straight season to either All-Star Team. It was the first time in seven seasons that

Maurice Richard had not been the First All-Star Team's right-winger.

Scored one goal in All-Star game as First All-Stars, augmented by players of United States Teams, and second All-Stars bolstered by Canadian Teams' players, tied 2–2. It was Howe's fourth straight All-Star game. He wore sweater number nine.

Received two assists, including his 300th point, as Red Wings and Toronto tied 2–2 at Detroit. It was his 342nd regular-season game.

Scored one goal at Toronto during a 3–1 Detroit victory. It was the eighth straight game in which Howe scored at least once — he had 10 goals during the streak, the longest consecutive goal-scoring streak of his career.

Assisted on Sid Abel's last goal as a Red Wing as Detroit defeated Toronto 6–2 at Detroit.

Scored three goals against netminder Gerry McNeil and had one assist as Detroit defeated Montreal 7–2 at Detroit. It was the last regular-season game for the Production Line and Sid Abel assisted on one of Howe's goals while Ted Lindsay assisted on another. Howe's assist was on a goal by Lindsay. Red Wings finished first for a fourth straight season, tying the record set by Boston twice and Montreal Canadiens once. Howe won his second straight scoring championship, tying his record of the previous season with 86 points, including a league-leading 47 goals.

Scored two goals, his only ones of the entire playoffs that season, and

had one assist in Wings' 3–0 victory over Montreal at Detroit.

Detroit defeated Montreal 3–0 at Detroit to win the Stanley Cup in an unprecedented eight straight games. It was Howe's second time on a Stanley Cup-winning team. The game also marked the final appearance of the Production Line with Sid Abel at center. Howe, with five assists, tied teammate Metro Prystai for the lead among all players in assists for the playoffs and his seven points tied him with Ted Lindsay, Floyd Curry of Montreal, and Prystai for the lead in points.

Named to the official NHL First All-Star Team for a second straight season, this time unanimously. It was his fourth berth on either team in as many seasons.

Won the Hart Memorial Trophy as the NHL's Most Valuable Player for the first time, becoming only the third Detroit player to receive the award. Ebbie Goodfellow won in 1939–40 and Sid Abel in 1948–49.

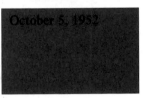

Played in his fifth straight All-Star game as the First All-Stars, of which Howe was a member, tied the Second All-Stars 1–1. Howe wore sweater number nine.

Received two assists as Detroit defeated Rangers 5–2 at New York. The first assist was on Ted Lindsay's 200th NHL regular-season goal and was also the 200th assist of Howe's regular-season career.

Scored one goal and had two assists, bringing his regular-season career total to 400 points in 413 games. Wings defeated Montreal 3–2 at Detroit.

February 15, 1953

Scored the 200th goal of his regular-season career against goaltender Al Rollins at 1:04 of the first period during a 4-1 win at Chicago.

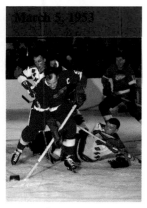
March 5, 1953

Scored a goal against goaltender Lorne Worsley at 16:36 of the second period on a penalty shot, the first of two such goals in his career. Howe scored another goal in the third period and had three assists in the game as Detroit defeated New York 7–1 at Detroit. The five points gave Howe 87 for the season, breaking the record he had set and tied in each of the two previous seasons.

March 19, 1953

Scored two goals in Wings' 6–1 victory against Boston at Detroit, leaving him with two games in which to score a goal to reach the 50-goal mark.

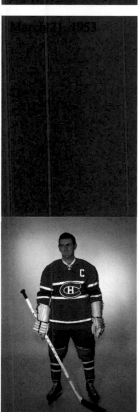
March 21, 1953

With left winger Bert Olmstead shadowing him, Howe failed in the final game of the season to score his 50th goal, which would have tied him for the record with Maurice Richard, who set the mark in 1944–45. Howe did, however finish the season with 49 goals, 46 assists and a record 95 points, which stood until 1958–59 when Dickie Moore of the Canadiens broke the mark with 96 points. Detroit and Montreal tied 1–1 at Detroit. For a record third straight season, Howe was the Art Ross Trophy winner. No player had ever won the scoring championship three times, let alone in consecutive seasons. The Wings, with another first-place finish, won the Prince of Wales Trophy for a record fifth straight season, Howe a member of all five. Howe, who led all players in goals and assists, finished 24 points ahead of

teammate and runner-up Ted Lindsay, the widest margin by which a player has ever won the scoring championship.

April 15, 1953

Married Colleen J. Joffa at Calvary Presbyterian Church on Grand River Avenue, Detroit, near the Olympia Stadium.

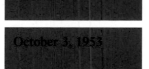
April 24, 1953

Named to the Official First NHL All-Star Team for the third straight season and a second year in a row unanimously. It was his fifth straight berth on either team.

March 5, 1953

Won the Hart Memorial Trophy for a second straight season.

October 3, 1953

Played in his sixth straight All-Star game as All-Stars defeated Canadiens 3–1 at Montreal.

November 28, 1953

Scored two goals during 9–0 win against Chicago at Detroit. Included was the game-winning goal, which meant that of five consecutive goals by Howe, from October 25, four were game-winning goals and the other was a game-tying goal.

February 14, 1954

Scored two goals and had one assist as Detroit won 5–0 at Chicago. Included was Howe's 500th regular-season point. It was Howe's 492nd regular-season game.

February 18, 1954

First son, Marty Gordon Howe, born.

March 10, 1954

Terry Sawchuk received an assist on a Howe goal, the first goaltender to assist Howe. Hank Bassen later received assists on two of Howe's goals — March 2, 1961, and January 27, 1963.

March 21, 1954

Scored one goal and had two

139

assists in final game of season — a 6–1 win over Toronto at Detroit — to earn his fourth straight scoring title and Art Ross Trophy. Howe finished with 33 goals, a league-leading 48 assists and 81 points. Detroit won its sixth straight league championship, Howe a member of all six.

April 1, 1954

Howe scored at the 0:09 mark against netminder Harry Lumley during a semi-final game won by Detroit 4–3 in overtime. It was the fastest goal ever scored from the start of a playoff game at the time. Also, Howe assisted on Ted Lindsay's goal at 1:01 of the second overtime period. The win moved Detroit into the Final Series against Montreal.

April 16, 1954

Tony Leswick's goal at 4:29 of overtime gave Detroit a 2–1 victory over Montreal at Detroit and the Stanley Cup for the second time in three years. It was the third time Howe had been on a Cup-winning team.

April 23, 1954

Named to the Official NHL First All-Star Team for fourth straight season. It was his sixth straight nomination for either team.

October 2, 1954

Appeared in seventh straight All-Star game and scored the game-tying goal as the Wings and All-Stars tied 2–2 at Detroit.

November 3, 1954

Suffered sprained shoulder during game at Toronto, which ended in 1–1 tie. The injury forced him to miss the next six games and ended a streak of 382 regular-season games.

December 1, 1954

Scored two goals, including the 250th of his regular-season career, as the Red Wings defeated Rangers 6–1 at New York. The

milestone goal was scored at 10:23 of the third period against goaltender Johnny Bower.

December 30, 1954

Scored two goals during 4–1 victory over Toronto at Detroit. The second was his 255th and made Howe the highest goal-scoring Red Wing in history, passing Ted Lindsay, who was out of action with an injury.

January 27, 1955

Had 19 shots on goal, setting a league record, but failed to get a goal as New York tied Detroit. Vic Howe, Gordie's younger brother, scored the game-tying goal at 11:57 of the third period. Lorne Worsley was the New York goaltender.

February 17, 1955

Received one assist during a 4–2 loss at Montreal. It was Howe's 300th regular-season assist.

March 20, 1955

Detroit defeated Montreal 6–0 at Detroit to win the seventh straight NHL championship and the Prince of Wales Trophy, Howe being on all seven.

April 10, 1955

Scored three goals — the only time in his career he did that in a playoff game — to lead the Red Wings to 5–1 victory over Canadiens at Montreal. The three goals boosted Howe's point total for the playoffs that season to 19, breaking the mark of 18 set by Toe Blake in 1943–44.

April 14, 1955

Scored the Stanley Cup-winning goal in a 3–1 victory over Montreal at Detroit in the seventh game of the finals. It was the Wings' second straight Stanley Cup title and the fourth for Howe. As it turned out, it was also the last time Howe was on a Cup-winning team. The goal was Howe's fifth

of the final round and ninth of the playoffs, giving him 20 points for the post season. Howe also recorded 12 points in the final series, a mark that was later tied (Jacques Lemaire and Yvan Cournoyer in 1973) and broken (13 points) by Wayne Gretzky in 1988.

April 22, 1955

All-Star Teams announced and for the first time in seven seasons, Howe was not named to either team — the only time in 22 consecutive seasons he did not gain a berth on either team.

May 28, 1955

Second son, Mark Steven Howe, born at Detroit Osteopathic Hospital. Dr. James Matthews assisted.

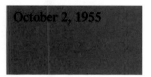
October 2, 1955

Scored one goal and had one assist as Detroit defeated All-Stars 3–1 at Detroit. It was Howe's eighth straight All-Star game appearance.

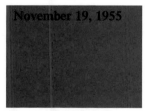
November 19, 1955

Scored two goals and had one assist in 4–1 victory against Chicago at Detroit. Included among the three points was his 600th regular-season point. It was his 591st regular-season game.

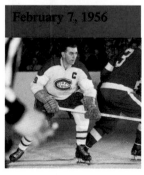
February 7, 1956

Scored two goals during 3–2 victory against Chicago at Detroit. His first, at 6:33 of the first period against goaltender Al Rollins, was the 300th regular-season goal of his career, making him only the third player to attain that plateau. Maurice Richard of Canadiens had 450 goals at that time and Nels Stewart retired with 324.

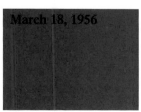
March 18, 1956

Detroit finished its regular schedule, a 2–0 loss to Toronto at Detroit. Howe did not get a point in the last three games, but finished the season with 38 goals, 41 assists and 79 points, good for second place in the

scoring race, nine points behind Jean Beliveau of Montreal.

April 17, 1956

Named to the Second All-Star Team, the seventh time in eight seasons he was chosen for either team.

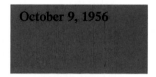
October 9, 1956

Missed his first All-Star game in nine years due to injury suffered during training camp. All-Stars tied Canadiens 1–1 at Montreal.

November 18, 1956

Assisted on Ted Lindsay's 300th regular-season NHL goal. It was scored at 7:51 of the second period during an 8–3 victory over Montreal at Detroit. Howe also had two goals and another assist in the game.

December 15, 1956

Scored two goals during 5–1 victory against Chicago at Detroit. The first, scored at 18:46 of the first period against goaltender Al Rollins, was the 325th goal of Howe's regular-season career, making him the second-highest goal scorer in NHL history by passing Nels Stewart's total of 324. Maurice Richard of Montreal led with 469 goals at this date.

December 5, 1956

Scored three goals and had three assists — the most points he recorded in one game in his 26-season career — during an 8–1 victory over New York at Detroit. Included was the 700th regular-season point of his career. He was playing his 673rd regular-season game.

February 7, 1957

Moved to center for a game because of an injury to regular center Norm Ullman. Ted Lindsay was at left wing and Metro Prystai, normally a center, to Howe's right wing spot. Boston shut out the Wings at Detroit, however, 1–0. Coach Jimmy Skinner explained:

"I've been curious about how Howe would look at center and this was a chance to find out."

March 9, 1957

Scored two goals, the second in his 350th in regular-season play, as Red Wings lost 4–2 at Boston. The milestone was at 13:17 of the second period against netminder Don Simmons.

March 14, 1957

Ted Lindsay, who had been a linemate regularly with Howe since November 1, 1947, received his last assist in regular-season play on a Howe goal as Detroit defeated Chicago 3–2 at Detroit. Lindsay received 147 regular-season assists on Howe goals.

March 24, 1957

Received two assists in final game of season — a 4–1 win against Toronto at Detroit — to boost his season's total to 89 points, including 44 goals and 45 assists, and win for him his fifth scoring championship and Art Ross Trophy. Howe's first assist in the game was on Ted Lindsay's last regular-season goal as a linemate of Howe. Lindsay was traded to Chicago before the start of the 1957–58 season. The Red Wings also finished first with 88 points, six more than runner-up Montreal for their eighth Prince of Wales Trophy title in nine seasons, of which Howe was a member each time.

March 28, 1957

Ted Lindsay received his final assist on a Howe goal — at 11:32 of the first period in the second game of the Detroit-Boston semifinal playoff series. Detroit won the game 7–2, but lost the series four games to one. Lindsay assisted on 12 of Howe's playoff goals.

April 4, 1957

Received his final playoff assist on

a Ted Lindsay goal at 36 seconds of the third period in the fifth and final game of a Boston-Detroit semifinal series. Boston won 4–3 to take the series. It was also the last time Howe and Lindsay were linemates.

April 23, 1957

Named to Official NHL First All-Star Team for a fifth time and his eighth selection to either team in nine seasons.

May 7, 1957

Winner of the Hart Memorial Trophy as the League's Most Valuable Player for the third time in his career.

October 5, 1957

Scored one goal in his ninth All-Star game in 10 years, as the All-Stars defeated Montreal 5–2 at Montreal.

November 20, 1957

Received one assist during 1–1 tie at New York, giving him a career total, including playoffs, of 454 assists, breaking the all-time record of 453 established by Elmer Lach of Montreal Canadiens.

November 28, 1957

Received one assist during a 3–3 tie with Toronto at Detroit to set an all-time record for career assists. He had 409 assists in regular-season play, eclipsing the mark of 400 established by Elmer Lach of Montreal Canadiens.

February 16, 1958

Scored one goal and received one assist during 4–1 win against Toronto at Detroit. The two points gave him a regular-season career total of 800 in 762 games.

April 29, 1958

Named to NHL First All-Star Team for a sixth time and his ninth selection to either team in 10 seasons.

May 13, 1958

Named winner of the Hart Memorial Trophy as the League's Most Valuable Player for the sec-

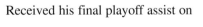

ond straight season and fourth time in his career, tying the record set by Eddie Shore, former great Boston defenseman.

Played in his 10th All-Star game in 11 years as Canadiens defeated the All-Stars 6–3 at Montreal.

First League game as captain of the Red Wings.

Scored the 400th goal of his regular-season career at 9:46 of the third period in Montreal. It was against netminder Jacques Plante and was the game-tying goal in a 2–2 tie. Pete Goegan and Norm Ullman received assists.

Because of weakness at defense through injuries, coach Sid Abel moved Howe to defense in a game won by Toronto 2–1 at Toronto. Howe first played defense during Detroit penalties and then played on a full-time basis in the third period. He also played right wing on his line with center Norm Ullman and left winger Alex Delvecchio.

Coach Sid Abel fined 14 Red Wings regulars $100 each following a 5–0 loss to New York at Detroit the night before. Included among those fined for "indifferent play" was Howe, who explained: "I didn't like getting fined but it will be worth $100 if the fines help us get into the playoffs."

"Gordie Howe Night" held at the Detroit Olympia to honor the 13-year veteran. Although he received $10,000 in gifts, the biggest thrill for Howe was the presence of his parents. It was the first time his father had seen Gordie play in an NHL arena. Howe didn't get a goal but received one assist in a 2–2 tie with Boston.

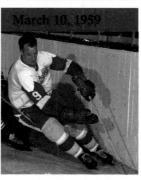

Scored two goals and had one assist to accomplish two milestones during 5–5 tie against Montreal at Detroit. The two goals gave him 30 for the season, the ninth time he had reached that figure, which tied the record set by Maurice Richard. The three points gave him 900 in regular-season play. It was his 84th regular-season game.

Red Wings lost their final game of the season 6–4 to Toronto at Detroit, and for the first time in Howe's career the Wings failed to gain a playoff berth. They finished with 58 points, seven from fourth-placed Toronto.

Third child, a daughter, Cathleen Jill Howe, born at Detroit Osteopathic Hospital. Dr. James Matthews assisted.

Named to the Second All-Star team, Howe's 10th selection to either team in 11 seasons.

Finished second behind Andy Bathgate of New York in the voting for the Hart Memorial Trophy.

Played in his 11th All-Star game in 12 seasons as Canadiens defeated the All-Stars 6–1 at Montreal.

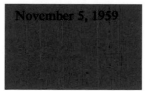

Scored one goal and had one assist during 8–3 loss to Boston at Detroit. The two points gave him 1,000 points, including playoffs. It was his 947th game, including playoffs.

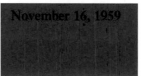

Received two assists during a 4–3 loss to Montreal at Detroit. That raised his career total to 500 assists in regular-season action.

January 16, 1960

Scored one goal and had one assist to become the NHL's all-time point-scoring leader, passing Maurice Richard. In a game at Detroit won by the Wings 3–1 against Chicago, Howe scored at 4:09 of the third period, assisted by Warren Godfrey and Murray Oliver. The two points came in Howe's 888th regular-season game while Richard scored his 949th point in the regular-season game.

March 8, 1960

Played in his 1,000th NHL game, including playoffs, during a 3–0 win over Montreal at Detroit.

March 20, 1960

Received one assist in Wings' final game of the season, a 3–2 loss to Toronto at Detroit. Howe finished with 28 goals, 45 assists and 73 points, which placed him sixth in the overall scoring list, the lowest he had finished in 11 seasons.

April 22, 1960

Named to NHL First All-Star Team for a seventh time and to either the First or Second Team for the 11th time in 12 seasons.

May 6, 1960

Winner of the Hart Memorial Trophy as the League's Most Valuable Player for a record fifth time.

September 15, 1960

Fourth child, Murray Albert Howe, born at Detroit Osteopathic Hospital. Dr. James Matthews assisted.

October 1, 1960

Played in his 12th All-Star game in 13 seasons as the All-Stars defeated the Canadiens 2–1 at Montreal.

November 6, 1960

Scored the 450th regular-season goal of his career during a 5–2 win against New York and goaltender Jack McCarten at Detroit. That left him 94 goals behind the regular-season record of 544 established by

Montreal's Maurice Richard, who retired after 18 seasons just before the start of the 1960–61 season.

November 20, 1960

Received the 1,000th point of his regular-season career when he assisted Howie Glover on a goal at 6:36 of the first period during a 2–0 win against Toronto at Detroit. It was his 938th regular-season game.

December 1, 1960

Assisted on a goal by Murray Oliver at 6:33 of the third period in a game at Detroit, won by Boston 3–2, giving him the record for most points, including playoffs. It was his 1,092nd point and his 1,034th game, both including playoffs. Maurice Richard of Montreal, who held the record, had 1,091 points in 1,111 games.

January 4, 1961

Collided with Eddie Shack during a game at Toronto and suffered a concussion which kept him out of four of the Wings' next five games. It was the first head injury suffered by Howe since his near-fatal accident in the playoffs of 1950.

February 8, 1961

Scored a goal during a 2–2 tie at Chicago, the 18th straight game in which he received at least one point. During the streak, he scored 10 goals and 17 assists for 27 points.

March 19, 1961

Failed to get a point in the final game of the season, finishing the season with 23 goals, 49 assists and 72 points. His goal total was his lowest in 12 seasons and only the first of two times since his third season that he did not reach the 25-goal mark.

April 8, 1961

Established an NHL record for most assists in playoff career when he received two during 3–1 win against Chicago at Detroit. He now had 61 assists, two more than Montreal defenseman Doug Harvey.

April 16, 1961

Received one assist at Detroit as Chicago defeated the Red Wings 5–1, the Hawks' first Stanley Cup in 23 years. The assist gave Howe 15 points for the playoffs and tied him with Chicago defenseman Pierre Pilote for the lead among all players that year.

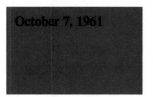

April 25, 1961

Named to the Second All-Star Team, the 12th time in 13 seasons he was voted to either the First or Second Team.

October 7, 1961

Scored one goal and had one assist as the All-Stars defeated the Blackhawks 31 at Chicago in Howe's 13th All-Star game in 14 seasons.

November 26, 1961

Became the first player in NHL history to play 1,000 regular-season games as Wings lost 4–1 at Chicago. Howe was held scoreless in the game. Ted Lindsay, during 15 seasons with Detroit and Chicago, had played 999 regular-season games.

November 30, 1961

Scored the winning goal in a 3–1 victory against Boston at Detroit. It was his 84th game winner of his career and broke the record of 83 set by Maurice Richard of Montreal in regular-season play.

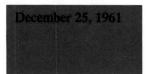

December 25, 1961

Received three assists, including the 600th of his regular-season career, as New York defeated the Wings 6–4 at Detroit.

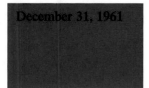

December 31, 1961

Scored three goals against goaltender Johnny Bower as Detroit defeated Toronto 4–2 at Detroit. The second goal, at 15:40 of the first period, was scored on a penal-

ty shot, the second and final such goal by Howe in his career.

January 21, 1962

Scored one goal as Canadiens defeated Wings 5–3 at Detroit. It was Howe's 1,100th regular-season point and came in his 1,023rd game.

March 14, 1962

Scored the 500th regular-season goal of his career at 17:10 of the second period, against netminder Lorne Worsley and assisted by Alex Delvecchio and Warren Godfrey. Rangers, however, won the game at New York, 3–2.

March 25, 1962

Scored only one goal as Canadiens defeated Detroit 5–2 in the final game of the season, and the Red Wings missed the play-offs for only the second time in Howe's career. Howe scored 33 goals for the season, the 10th time he reached 30 or more goal seasons. Howe resigned as captain of the Wings and Alex Delvecchio was named his successor.

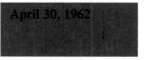

April 30, 1962

Named to Second All-Star Team, the 13th time in 14 seasons he had been selected to either team.

October 6, 1962

Scored All-Stars' long goal in a 4–1 loss to the Maple Leafs at Toronto. It was Howe's 14th All-Star game in 15 years, breaking the record of 13 he shared with Maurice Richard of Montreal.

March 5, 1963

Scored one goal, his 1,200th point in regular-season play, in the Wings' 4–3 loss to Montreal at Detroit. It was his 1,112th regular-season goal.

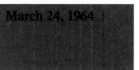

March 24, 1964

Scored one goal and had one assist as Detroit defeated Toronto 3–2 at Detroit. The two points gave Howe 86 for the season, including

a League-leading 38 goals, and his sixth scoring championship and Art Ross Trophy.

April 18, 1963

Toronto defeated Red Wings 3–1 at Toronto in the seventh game of the Stanley Cup Final to win the Championship. Howe had one assist in the game, giving him 16 points for the playoffs and tying him with teammate Norm Ullman as co-leaders of all players in play-off points that year.

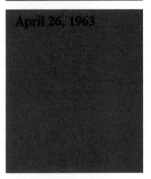

April 26, 1963

Named to NHL First All-Star Team for an eighth time and to either team for the 14th time in 15 seasons, which tied Maurice Richard's record for most All-Star berths. Eight of Richard's selections were also First Team berths. Doug Harvey, defenseman with Montreal and New York, held the record of 10 First Team choices.

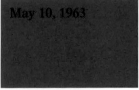

May 10, 1963

Winner of the Hart Memorial Trophy as NHL's Most Valuable Player for a sixth time. Only Wayne Gretzky has won it more often (nine times).

October 5, 1963

Played in his 15th All-Star game in 16 seasons; All-Stars and Toronto tied 3–3 at Toronto. He received one assist to break the record for most points in All-Star game action. Howe's assist was the 11th point. He and Ted Lindsay, who played in 11 games while with Detroit and Chicago, had shared the record of 10 points each. Howe and Maurice Richard were tied for the lead in goals with seven each. All-Star coach Sid Abel had one of the most potent power-plays ever assembled: Jean Beliveau at center, Bobby Hull at left wing, Gordie Howe at right wing, Bernie Geoffrion and Andy Bathgate on the points.

October 27, 1963

Scored a record-tying 544th regular-season goal at 100:04 of the third period in a game against net-minder Lorne Worsley and Montreal at Detroit. Bill Gadsby and Bruce MacGregor assisted on the power-play goal. Canadiens won the game 6–4.

November 10, 1963

Moved past Maurice Richard of Montreal as the all-time goal-scoring leader in regular-season play as he beat goaltender Charlie Hodge at 15:06 of the second period in a 3–0 win against Montreal at Detroit. Billy McNeill assisted Howe on the shorthand goal. It came in Howe's 1,132nd regular-season game, while Richard scored 544 goals in 978 regular-season games. The shutout recorded by Terry Sawchuk tied the record for all-time lead in shutouts, Hainsworth and Sawchuk each with 94. Sawchuk broke the record January 19, 1964, at Montreal when the Red Wings won 2–0.

February 2, 1964

Received one assist, the 700th of his regular-season career, during a 2–2 tie with Toronto at Detroit.

April 5, 1964

Scored one goal during a 3–2 loss at Chicago in the fifth game of the Semi-Final Series. It was the 127th point of his playoff career and broke the record of 126 set by Maurice Richard of Montreal, who had 82 goals and 44 assists in 133 games. Howe's 127th point was in the 122nd game.

April 25, 1964

Detroit was defeated 4–0 at Toronto in the deciding game of the Stanley Cup Final but Howe, for the sixth and final time of his career, led all point scorers with 19 and for the third time led all goal scorers with nine.

April 30, 1964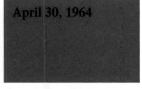

Named to the Second All-Star Team for the seventh time. It was the 15th selection to either team in 16 years, thus breaking the record he shared with Maurice Richard.

October 10, 1964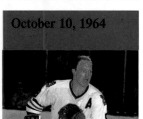

Coach Sid Abel had a "dream line" for the All-Star game — Howe at right wing, Jean Beliveau at center and Bobby Hull at left wing. The line scored one goal — Beliveau, assisted by Hull and Howe — as the All-Stars defeated Toronto 3–2 at Toronto. It was Howe's 16th All-Star Game in 17 years.

October 18, 1964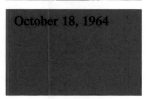

Scored two goals and added one assist during a 3–2 win against Chicago at Detroit. Included was his 1,200th point which came in his 1,192nd regular-season game.

November 14, 1964

Became the all-time goal-scoring leader, including playoffs, when he beat netminder Charlie Hodge at the 20-second mark of the first period during a 4–2 victory at Montreal. it was his 627th goal, 570 during the regular-season and 57 in the playoffs, and was scored in his 1,233rd game, including playoffs. Maurice Richard had scored 626 goals — 544 regular-season and 82 playoff in 1,111 games, including playoffs. Howe now held all offensive career records — most goals; most goals including playoffs; most assists; most assists including playoffs; most points; and most point including playoffs.

November 15, 1964

Assisted, for the final time, a goal by Ted Lindsay, who had come out of retirement for one season. It was the only time the two former linemates combined for a goal that season. Detroit won the game 6–2 at New York.

March 25, 1965

Alex Delvecchio scored three goals during a 7–4 Red Wing win against New York at Detroit. It was the third straight game in which a Detroit player scored three goals in a game — Norm Ullman scoring three against New York in a 6–6 tie at New York, March 19th, and Howe scoring three goals against Chicago in a 5–1 win at Detroit, March 21st.

March 28, 1965

Wings shut out 4–0 by Toronto at Detroit but finished first to win their ninth Prince of Wales Trophy title in 17 seasons, Howe a member of all nine.

April 4, 1965

Scored the fourth and final short-handed goal of his playoff career during a 6–3 Semi-Final Series win against Chicago. He also scored the winning goal in the game, his 10th and final of his playoff career. He never scored an overtime goal.

May 7, 1965

Named to Second All-Star Team for the eighth time and his 16th selection to either team in 17 years.

October 20, 1965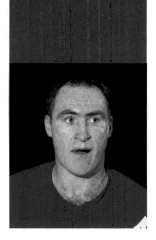

Played in his 17th All-Star game in 18 seasons; scored two goals and had two assists to set two records and tie three others as the All-Stars defeated Canadiens 5–2 at Montreal. The two goals were his eighth and ninth in All-Star competition. He had a goal and two assists in the second period, a record for most points in a period. His assists tied him with Red Kelly, each with seven in All-Star competition. His four points in one game tied the record set by teammate Ted Lindsay in the 9–5 game at Detroit.

November 27, 1965	Scored his 600th regular-season goal at 16:10 of the third period. It was against netminder Lorne Worsley at Montreal during a Canadiens 3–2 victory. Gary Bergman and Don McKenney assisted.
December 15, 1965	Andy Bathgate scored the 300th goal of his regular-season career, Howe and Alex Delvecchio assisting. Detroit lost the game 5–3 at Toronto.
January 15, 1966	Received one assist, the 1,400th point of his regular-season career as the Red Wings and New York tied 4–4 at Detroit. It was Howe's 1,295th game.
January 25, 1966	Played his 1,300th regular-season game and received one assist as Wings lost at New York 4–3.

February 3, 1965 — Alex Delvecchio scored the 300th goal of his regular-season career and Howe assisted as Detroit won at Boston 4–2. At the time, nine players had scored 300 or more goals in their careers and Howe was involved directly with four of the 300th goals — his own, and those of Ted Lindsay, Andy Bathgate, and Alex Delvecchio, each of whom Howe assisted on their milestone goals. The other 300-or-more goal scorers were Maurice Richard, Jean Beliveau, Bernie Geoffrion, Nels Stewart and Bobby Hull.

February 13, 1966	Scored one goal and received two assists, including the 800th regular-season assist of his career, as Montreal defeated the Red Wings 4–3 at Detroit.
May 5, 1966	Montreal defeated Detroit 3-2 after 2:20 of overtime to win the Stanley Cup. It was Howe's last final series playoff.

May 12, 1966	Named to the Official NHL First All-Star Team for the ninth time and to either team for the 17th time in 18 years.

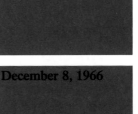

July 22, 1966 — "Gordie Howe Day" in Saskatoon, Saskatchewan, which attracted at least half the city and many hockey people from all over to honor the city's top ambassador. One of the highlights was the reunion of the entire Howe family, including Gordie's three brothers and five sisters — their first time home together in 18 years.

October 19, 1966	Had one assist in a 6–2 loss at Boston. This was the first game of his 21st consecutive season in the NHL, breaking the record he held with former Boston great, Dit Clapper, and Bill Gadsby, who played 20 seasons with Chicago, New York and Detroit.
December 8, 1966	Scored one goal and had an assist as Rangers defeated the Red Wings 4–2 at Detroit. It was Howe's 1,500th NHL game, including playoffs.
January 5, 1967	Scored two goals as Wings defeated Chicago 6–4 at Detroit. The second goal was Howe's 700th, including playoffs.
January 18, 1967	Appeared in his 18th All-Star game in 19 seasons as Canadiens defeated the All-Stars 3–0 at Montreal.
March 18, 1967	Out of action with a bruised shoulder, Howe made his NHL coaching debut as he went behind the bench while coach Sid Abel observed the game from the press box. Wings lost, however, to Boston 5–3 at Detroit. Howe returned to the Detroit line-up on his regular right wing position the next game.

March 28, 1967 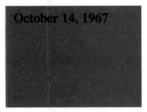	Received one assist during a 7–2 loss at Chicago. It was the 1,500th point for Howe and came in his 1,369th game.
May 10, 1967	Voted an All-Star for the 18th time in 19 seasons, this time to the Second Team. It was the 12th straight season he was chosen to either team.
October 14, 1967	Scored against netminder Rogatien Vachon at 15:17 of the second period, during a 6–2 loss at Montreal. Gary Jarrett and Alex Delvecchio assisted on the goal, Howe's 650th in regular-season play.
January 16, 1968	Received one assist as the Leafs defeated the All-Stars 4–3 at Toronto. It was Howe's 19th All-Star game appearance in 20 seasons.
March 31, 1968 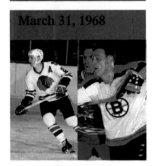	Received one assist in Detroit's final game of the season, a 5–5 tie at Chicago. Howe scored 39 goals and had 43 assists for 82 points, which placed him third in the scoring parade, only five points from champion Stan Mikita of Chicago and two behind runner-up Phil Esposito of Boston.
May 16, 1968	Named to the NHL First All-Star Team for a 10th time, tying the record set by Doug Harvey. It was Howe's nineteenth selection to either team in 20 years.
October 31, 1968	Received three assists including his 900th during the regular season, as Wings defeated Boston 7–5 at Detroit.
November 7, 1968	Received one assist, the 1,600th point of his career, as the Wings defeated Minnesota 5–2 at Detroit. It was Howe's 1,482nd regular-season.

November 10, 1968	Received one assist, the 1,000th of his career including playoffs, in a 4–4 tie with Montreal at Detroit.
December 4, 1968 	Scored the 700th regular-season goal of his career. It was at 7:13 of the first period against netminder Les Binkley during a 7–2 win at Pittsburgh. Frank Mahovlich and Alex Delvecchio assisted.
January 21, 1969	Appeared in his 20th All-Star game in 21 seasons, playing on a line with Bobby Hull and Phil Esposito. He did not receive a point.
January 25, 1969	Scored one goal during a 5–3 win over Oakland at Detroit. It was the 1,000th point of his career, including playoffs. It was his 1,669th game, including playoffs.
March 16, 1969	Scored his 40th goal of the season during a 6–4 loss at New York. It was the fifth and final time he reached that figure.
March 19, 1969	Scored one goal and received one assist for a record-breaking 96 points by a right winger in one season. Howe held the old mark of 95. The points were during a 4–4 tie at Oakland.
March 30, 1969 	Scored two goals and received two assists in the final game of the season, a 9–5 loss at Chicago. That gave him 59 assists for the season, a record for a right winger, breaking the old mark of 58 by Andy Bathgate. His 103 points, including 44 goals, was also a record for points by a right winger. He was one of three players to top the 100-point mark, the first time this had been accomplished. Phil Esposito won the scoring title with 126 points, followed by Bobby Hull with 107. His assists and points

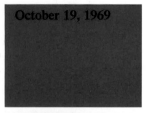

were broken by Ken Hodge of Boston in 1970–71.

May 9, 1969

Named to the NHL First All-Star Team for a record-breaking 11th time and to either team for the 20th time in 21 years. It was also his 14th straight selection to either team, tying the record set by Maurice Richard.

October 19, 1969

Scored an empty-net goal at 19:19 of the third period while Red Wings were shorthanded during a 4–2 victory against St. Louis at Detroit. It was the 800th goal of his career, including playoffs.

November 2, 1969

Scored three goals against goaltender Al Smith during a 4–3 win against Pittsburgh at Detroit. It was his 19th and final three-goal game.

November 27, 1969

Received two assists in a 5–1 win against Los Angeles at Detroit. The first was the 1,700th point of his career and was gained in his 1,567th game.

December 25, 1969

For the first time in 16 years, Howe was able to be home for Christmas since Detroit was not scheduled to play between December 21st and 26th.

January 20, 1970

Scored the game-winning goal as the East All-Stars defeated the West All-Stars 4–1 at St. Louis. A power-play goal, the other players on the ice from the east at the time were Bobby Orr, Phil Esposito, Jacques Lemaire and Bobby Hull.

February 8, 1970

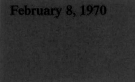

Scored the 750th regular-season goal of his career, at 3:10 of the third period against netminder Bernie Parent during Philadelphia's 5–3 win at Detroit. Alex Delvecchio

and Wayne Connelly assisted on the power-play goal.

March 7, 1970

Scored the 16th and final empty-net goal of his career at 19:57 of the third period in a 4–2 win at Montreal.

April 4, 1970

Scored two goals in a 6–2 victory against New York at Detroit. They were his 39th and 40th goals of the season and gave him a record 14 30-or-more-goal seasons.

April 5, 1970

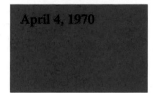

Scored one goal as he appeared in the first game of his final playoff year. It marked a record-tying 19th year in the playoffs, the same as Red Kelly. The two still share the record. Chicago won the game, at Chicago, 4–2.

April 12, 1970

Scored his final goal and final point as a Red Wing in playoff competition as Chicago defeated the Wings 4–2 at Detroit to eliminate them from the playoffs. Howe had a playoff career record with Detroit of 154 games, which was second at the time to Red Kelly's 164; 67 goals, third at the time to Maurice Richard (82) and Jean Beliveau (73); 91 assists, a record at the time but since broken by Beliveau; 158 points, also a record at the time but also since broken by Beliveau.

May 21, 1970

Named to the Official NHL First All-Star Team for a record 12th time. It was the 15th straight season he had been named to either team, breaking the record held by Maurice Richard. Eight of those 15 selections were to the First Team. Altogether, Howe was picked to either team a record 21 times. He missed only once in 22 straight seasons. The $2,000 he received for the First Team Selection on this date brought his total earnings from League awards — including All-Star nominations, his share of team awards, and trophy titles — to $78,925, over 24 seasons, an average of $3,288.54 per season.

June 1970

Bone ending removed from his left wrist at University of Michigan Hospital.

October 10, 1970

Began his 25th and final season in Detroit uniform as the Red Wings defeated California 5–3 at home. Howe received one assist.

October 29, 1970

Scored one goal and had two assists, including the 1,000th of his regular-season career, as Red Wings defeated Boston 5–3 at Detroit.

November 22, 1970

Scored twice and had one assist during a 4–2 victory at Philadelphia, but suffered a rib injury that kept him out of the next ten games. It was the longest absence from action for Howe since he missed 20 games in 1948–49. If he had not missed one game in 1963–64 and another in 1966–67, he would have played 690 consecutive games.

January 19, 1971

Appeared in his 22nd All-Star game in 23 years and his 14th consecutive game. He shared the previous mark with Maurice Richard. At the time, he had six All-Star game records and shared two others. The West All-Stars defeated the East All-Stars in the game 2–1, played at Boston.

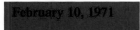

January 30, 1971

Scored his 29th and final game-tying goal as Los Angeles and the Red Wings tied 3–3 at Detroit.

February 10, 1971

Alex Delvecchio was credited with his final assist on a Gordie

Howe goal as Wings lost 5–2 at Los Angeles. Delvecchio led all players in assists on Howe's goals with 209 in regular-season and 20 in playoffs.

February 17, 1971

Played on a line with his two sons, Marty and Mark, in a March of Dimes benefit game at Detroit Olympia, during a 6–6 tie with the Detroit Junior Red Wings.

February 18, 1971

Scored his 20th goal of the season as Detroit defeated Minnesota 5–3 at Detroit. It was also Howe's 850th goal including playoffs and his 118th and final game-winning goal. It was the 22nd straight season that Howe reached the 20-goal mark, a record. Second best was Maurice Richard of Montreal who had 14 straight 20-or-more-goal seasons.

February 20, 1971

Scored one goal and three assists in a 6–5 win over Buffalo at Detroit. Included was the 1,800th regular-season point, coming in his 1,670th game.

March 18, 1971

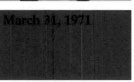

Assisted for the final time on a goal by Alex Delvecchio. The two had played on the same line regularly since 1958–59. Detroit lost at Boston 7–3.

March 31, 1971

Received 1,023rd and final assist. It was on a goal by Arnie Brown at 17:01 of the first period during a 2–2 tie at Toronto.

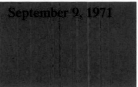

June 25, 1971

Received the Order of Canada Medal of Honour for distinguished service to sports and citizenship.

September 9, 1971

Announced his retirement as an active player at a news luncheon in a downtown Detroit hotel. The Red Wings announced that sweater number 9 would be retired

permanently — with one exception: if one of Gordie's sons played with Detroit. Howe's final totals with Detroit read, including playoffs, 1,841 games, 853 goals, 1,114 assists, and 1,967 points.

1970–72	Served as a vice president of the Detroit Hockey Club in Public Relations.
1971	Named to the Saskatchewan Sports Hall of Fame in Regina.
September 16, 1971	Named Hockey Player of the Last Quarter Century by *Sport* magazine in its poll for leading athletes of the last 25 years.
June 7, 1972	Named to Hockey Hall of Fame in Toronto. This was the first time female family members were allowed to attend ceremony or luncheon.

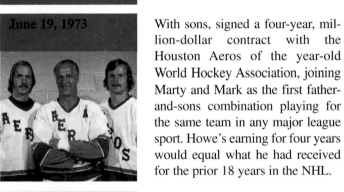

June 19, 1973	With sons, signed a four-year, million-dollar contract with the Houston Aeros of the year-old World Hockey Association, joining Marty and Mark as the first father-and-sons combination playing for the same team in any major league sport. Howe's earning for four years would equal what he had received for the prior 18 years in the NHL.
1973	World Hockey Association honored Howe by establishing a league award and bronze trophy in his name.
June 1974	Became leader of playoff assists and earned Most Valuable Player in his first comeback season.
1974	Along with sons, played on the Canadian All-Star team that played eight games against the Soviets in international competi-

tion. The father/sons combination was a first in sports history.

June 1975– September 1976	Became the first playing club president in major league sports.
March 2, 1977	Scored his 900th major league goal.
June 4, 1977	Marty Gordon Howe wed Mary James in Houston, Texas.
July 9, 1977	Mark Steven Howe wed Virginia (Ginger) Lowery in Houston, Texas.
May 23, 1977	Signed a long-term contract with sons to play for the New England Whalers of the WHA.
December 7, 1977	Scored his 1,000th career goal in professional hockey against goaltender John Garrett of the Birmingham Bulls at Birmingham, Alabama, at 18:24 of the first period.
April 21, 1978	First grandchild, Travis Gordon Howe, born in Hartford, Connecticut. Howe was in Edmonton that night and scored a goal in the game with Mark, Travis's dad.
1978–79 season	Missed 22 games because of hairline fracture of his ankle bone.
August 5, 1978	Cathleen Jill Howe wed Daniel James Greer in Kalamazoo, Michigan (later divorced).

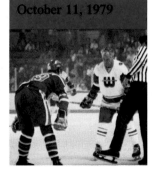

October 11, 1979	Returned to the NHL after an eight-year absence, skating for the Hartford Whalers in the club's first-ever NHL game. Howe's sons, Marty and Mark, also dressed for Whalers, marking the first time an NHL team had ever fielded a father-son combination in the line-up. All three Howes were held scoreless as Hartford lost 4–1 at Minnesota.

 **October 22, 1979**

Second grandchild, Jaime Elizabeth Greer, born in Kalamazoo, Michigan, to daughter Cathleen.

 **October 31, 1979**

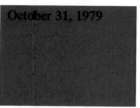

Scored his first goal in a Whalers uniform and his first in League play since April 6, 1971, in the NHL, in a 3–3 tie at Pittsburgh. Howe beat goaltender Greg Millen at 10:23 of the first period, with assist going to Al Sims and Mike Antonvich.

October 31, 1979

Scored his third goal of the season, assisted by son Mark and Al Hangsleben, to help Hartford defeat Toronto 4–1. It marked the first time that one of the Howes had set up the other's goal.

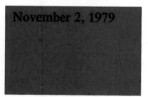 **November 2, 1979**

Recorded the only three-point night of the season in a 5–3 home win over Toronto. Howe had two goals and one assist against Leafs goaltender Mike Palmateer.

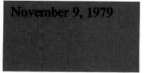 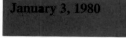 **November 9, 1979**

Appeared in his 13th game of the season and 1,700th regular-season game of his career, becoming the first player ever to reach that level.

January 3, 1980

Became the first 50-year-old to play major league hockey.

 **February 5, 1980**

Returned to the Motor City for his 23rd All-Star appearance before a record-breaking crowd of 21,000 at Detroit's Joe Louis Arena. He collected his 19th and final All-Star point, an assist on Real Cloutier's tally to conclude a four-goal Wales Conference outburst late in the third period, as the Wales defeated the Campbell Conference 5–3.

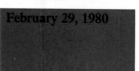 **February 29, 1980**

Became first player ever to record 800 career goals. The milestone tally, assisted by Greg Carroll and Bernie Johnston, came in a 3–0

shutout over the St. Louis Blues and goaltender Mike Liut.

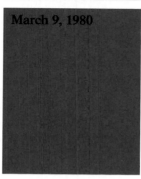 **March 9, 1980**

Realized a lifelong dream by playing alongside sons Marty and Mark in an NHL game. While Gordie and Mark were appearing in their 65th and 62nd games of the season, respectively, Marty was making his Whaler and NHL debut. None of the three Howes reached the scoresheet, as Hartford tied the Bruins 1–1 at Boston Gardens.

 **April 9, 1980**

Scored one goal and added one assist in Hartford's 8–4 loss to Montreal in Game 2 of their Preliminary Round Series. the two points were his last in the NHL play, the 2,009th and 2,010th of his career, including playoffs.

 **April 11, 1980**

Appeared in his last NHL game as Hartford was eliminated from the playoffs by Montreal Canadiens in three games. Including playoffs, Howe appeared in 1,924 games, with scoring totals of 869 goals and 1,141 assists for 2,010 points.

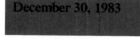 **December 1, 1981**

Third grandchild, Azia Candace Howe, born in Hartford, Connecticut, son Mark's child.

 **December 30, 1983**

Murray Albert Howe married Colleen Moore in Canton, Michigan.

 **May 4, 1985**

Cathleen Jill Howe married Wade Alan Roskam, Traverse City, Michigan, second marriage.

 **March 24, 1986**

Fourth grandchild, Nolan Gerry Howe, born in Houston, Texas. Mark's third child.

 **June 17, 1987**

Fifth grandchild, Jade Marie Roskam, born in Rochester, Michigan. Cathleen's second child.

December 26, 1987 — Sixth grandchild, Meaghan Colleen Howe, born in Detroit, Michigan. Murray's first child.

July 9, 1989 — Seventh grandchild, Gordon Moore Howe, born in Detroit, Michigan. Murray's second child.

May 3, 1992 — Eighth grandchild, Corey Howe, born in Toledo, Ohio. Murray's third child.

VIII - Career Stats

GP = Games Played, G = Goals, A = Assists, PTS = Points, PIM = Penalties in Minutes

Year	Team	League	Regular Season					Playoffs				
			GP	G	A	PTS	PIM	GP	G	A	PTS	PIM
1944-45	Galt Red Wings	OHA	—	—	—	—	—	—	—	—	—	—
1945-46	Omaha Knights	USHL	51	22	25	48	53	6	2	1	3	15
1946-47	Detroit Red Wings	NHL	58	7	15	22	52	5	0	0	0	18
1947-48	Detroit Red Wings	NHL	60	16	28	44	63	10	1	1	2	11
1948-49	Detroit Red Wings	NHL	40	12	25	37	57	11	8	3	11	19
1949-50	Detroit Red Wings	NHL	70	35	33	68	69	1	0	0	0	7
1950-51	Detroit Red Wings	NHL	70	43	43	86	74	6	4	3	7	4
1951-52	Detroit Red Wings	NHL	70	47	39	86	78	8	2	5	7	2
1952-53	Detroit Red Wings	NHL	70	49	46	95	57	6	2	5	7	2
1953-54	Detroit Red Wings	NHL	70	33	48	81	109	12	4	5	9	31
1954-55	Detroit Red Wings	NHL	64	29	33	62	68	11	9	11	20	24
1955-56	Detroit Red Wings	NHL	70	38	41	79	100	10	3	9	12	8
1956-57	Detroit Red Wings	NHL	70	44	45	89	72	5	2	5	7	6
1957-58	Detroit Red Wings	NHL	64	33	44	77	40	4	1	1	2	0
1958-59	Detroit Red Wings	NHL	70	32	36	78	57	-	-	-	-	-
1959-60	Detroit Red Wings	NHL	70	28	45	73	46	6	1	5	6	4
1960-61	Detroit Red Wings	NHL	64	23	49	72	30	11	4	11	15	10
1961-62	Detroit Red Wings	NHL	70	33	44	77	54	-	-	-	-	-
1962-63	Detroit Red Wings	NHL	70	38	48	86	100	11	7	9	16	22
1963-64	Detroit Red Wings	NHL	69	26	47	73	70	14	9	10	19	16
1964-65	Detroit Red Wings	NHL	70	29	47	76	104	7	4	2	6	20
1965-66	Detroit Red Wings	NHL	70	29	46	75	83	12	4	6	10	12
1966-67	Detroit Red Wings	NHL	69	25	40	65	53	-	-	-	-	-
1967-68	Detroit Red Wings	NHL	74	39	43	82	53	-	-	-	-	-
1968-69	Detroit Red Wings	NHL	76	44	59	103	58	-	-	-	-	-
1969-70	Detroit Red Wings	NHL	76	31	40	71	58	4	2	0	2	2
1970-71	Detroit Red Wings	NHL	63	23	29	52	38	-	-	-	-	-
1973-74	Houston Aeros	WHA	70	31	69	100	46	13	3	14	17	34
1974-75	Houston Aeros	WHA	75	34	65	99	84	13	8	12	20	20
1975-76	Houston Aeros	WHA	78	32	70	102	76	17	4	8	12	31
1976-77	Houston Aeros	WHA	62	24	44	68	57	11	5	3	8	11
1977-78	New England Whalers	WHA	76	34	62	96	85	14	5	5	10	15
1978-79	New England Whalers	WHA	58	19	24	43	51	10	3	1	4	4
1979-80	Hartford Whalers	NHL	80	15	26	41	42	3	1	1	2	2
	NHL Totals		1,767	801	1,049	1,850	1,685	157	68	92	160	220
	WHA Totals		419	174	334	508	399	78	28	43	71	115
	Major League Totals		2,186	975	1,383	2,358	2,084	235	96	135	231	355
	Regular & Playoff Totals		2,421	1,071	1,518	2,589	2,419					

Awards

Art Ross Trophy	1950-51, 1951-52, 1952-53, 1953-54, 1956-57, 1962-63
First All-Star Team Right Wing	1950-51, 1951-52, 1952-53, 1953-54, 1956-57, 1957-58, 1959-60, 1962-63, 1965-66, 1967-68, 1968-69, 1969-70
Hart Memorial Trophy	1951-52, 1952-53, 1956-57, 1957-58, 1959-60, 1962-63
Lester Patrick Trophy	1966-67
Second All-Star Team Right Wing	1948-49, 1949-50, 1955-56, 1958-59, 1960-61, 1963-64, 1964-65, 1966-67